Indian Folk Literature

Origin, Growth and Modern Appeal

Indian Folk Literature

Origin, Growth and Modern Appeal

Edited by

Suman Bala

Sandeep Pathak

Prestige Books International

New Delhi

Published by
Prestige Books International
New Delhi 110 060
prestigebooks@gmail.com
Phone: 9818755529

Associate Office
11B, Broomwood Road
London SW11 6HU

Associate Office
P.O. Box 2250
Sydney 2001

ISBN: 978-81-943008-0-8

Printed in India

Contents

Creative Writing

Indian Folk Literature: Introduction

SUMAN BALA and SANDEEP PATHAK

Folklore has ancient roots and offers a rich legacy to us in the present times. The generation today is missing the charm and innocence that these stories carry within them. It was at the end of the nineteenth century that interest in folk legends and poetry began but in the recent years, technology has overtaken this trend and relegated it to the background. It is high time that we pay attention to the variety and richness of folk literature. Folk legends, stories and poetry have a charm of their own. The present volume is devoted to revive interest in this genre by discussing various aspects related to definition, form, theme and variety in this area.

II

What is folklore? In simple terms, folklore is a combination of the words 'folk' and 'lore' which dates back to 1846. The former refers to a community of people, and the latter comes from the old English 'lar' which means knowledge. The comparative study of folk knowledge and culture is called 'folkloristics.' Folklore literature presents traditional customs, tales, sayings, dances, or art forms preserved among a set of people. These include oral traditions such as tales, proverbs and even jokes.

It is interesting to note that folklore is not taught in a formal school or college curriculum. It is passed along informally from one individual to another through verbal conversation. The academic study of folklore is called Folklore Literature or Folklore Studies.

Yet another means of dissemination of folktales is the wandering sadhus and fakirs. The sadhus with their saffron robes seek shelter and food in the villages; they are welcomed by the villagers, particularly by young children who collect around them and listen to the stories with rapt attention.

Mothers and grandmothers resort to telling folktales while feeding children at home. They narrate stories to distract the child's attention and the child is lured to happily accept the food. These tales also help mothers to persuade defiant children to make them come to terms with the advice of the seniors.

The folktales are narrated by both men and women. Mostly the elderly people narrate these stories to the young. The listeners usually sit in a semi-circle and enjoy the stories spellbound. These people are known as 'Kathasagar' in the villages. In some areas, the folktales are set to music. The stories are told in songs. This is common among tribals.

III

One of the landmarks in the area of folk literature was the publication of the book *Folktales of India*, edited by Brenda E.F. Beck et al. It has an elaborate Foreword by eminent Indian scholar and poet A.K. Ramanujan. The collection and translation of Indian oral tales began over more than a hundred years ago. About 3000 oral tales from Indic region, including Sri Lanka, Pakistan and Bangladesh were available in translation to the English reader in the year 1919. The study of Indian folklore enjoyed immense popularity, as India was thought to be the original motherland of all European folk narratives. Over the years, folk literature gained popularity and now so much attention is being paid to it by academics and Indologists.

In order to evaluate folk literature in Asia, we need to assess the literatures of major countries in the region. Within Asian and predominantly Hindu literature, we find the values, morality, humanity and principles of right human conduct that help human beings live a harmonious, peaceful and moral life. In nutshell, Asian literature is a compendium of ideas where culture, belief, religion and values collide. These are of intrinsic value to all of us. There are, for example, many parallels and similarities between folk literature of India and China, in terms of its origin and growth as also in its social and spiritual heritage. There are certain tribes, both in India and China, who are still leading a primitive life. The existence of this great diversity of folk cultures is an interesting phenomenon that makes a rich contribution to the corpus of Asian civilization. In the history of China, says eminent folklorist Zhong Jingwen, "the development of folk literature and art as part of life can be traced back to monolithic times, and its progress can be charted alongside the advancement of society." (6)

As society underwent transformation with the spread of education, scholars of upper class started looking upon folk literature with some kind of disdain. They considered it inferior, not on par with serious and sublime literature. With the founding of New China in 1949, there was resurgence of interest in folk literature. It was during this time that Tibetan epic *Khan Gesar*, the world's longest epic poem, was produced. Like the outstanding Greek and Indian epics, *King Gesar* is a brilliant pearl in the world's social and cultural treasure. It is a fascinating study of mythology and legend that reflects the society of the time.

Folktales are artistic creations handed down by the ordinary people of nation. This is true of both India and China. These tales highlight the collective wisdom and strength of the people. Giving vent to the true-to-the life experiences, they sometimes plunge the reader straight into the bizarre world of magic and mystery; through our willing suspension of disbelief. Coleridge strongly held the view that when a writer or episode infuses 'human interest and semblance of truth' into a fantastic tale, the readers or audience easily suspend their logical faculty.

Although folklore is probably as old as mankind, the term 'Folklore' is of comparatively recent origin. Interest in what we call folklore had existed long before the subject acquired its modern name. A great deal of research was done by European scholars in the seventeenth and eighteenth centuries: Robert Burton, John Brand, Johann Gottfried Von Herder and Jacob Grimm. Folk studies grew over the years and by the end of the 19th century, it became an independent branch of knowledge. Folklore research is conducted to record and describe traditional art, oral literature, beliefs, material objects, culture and customs.

Folklore deals mainly with the systematic and scientific analytic study of folk materials. In India, folklore studies began with the setting up of the Royal Asiatic Society of Bengal, in 1774. In the recent decades, A.K. Ramanujan has been hailed as a noted folklorist who analyzed folklore in Indian context.

The folk literature of a country belongs to its common people whose thoughts and feelings are embedded in it in the most native, down-to-earth and spontaneous manner. The folktales are deeply rooted in their social environment and have lasting appeal being lucid, entertaining and engaging.

Max Mueller, the German Indologist, interpreted the common pattern in folk literature as evidence of nature-myths. In his book *Folk Tales of Maharashtra*, the scholar I. Sheorey traces the growth of folklore in India and states that "the study of folklore in India is of very recent origin. This is all the more regrettable because the *Panchatantra* had spread through various channels almost throughout the world."

It was at the end of the nineteenth century that interest in folk poetry and legends began. Folk songs fascinated one and all. It also received attention from sociologists, Indologists and anthropologists. It is interesting to note that there is a strong trend in favour of women in the field of oral tradition songs, poems and religious incantations.

The range of folktales is wide. Apart from social, political, domestic themes, there are abundant fairy tales that have become popular both in the East and the West. Majority of these tales are common between India and Europe, especially England, France and Germany. According to one school of thought, the origin of these tales is India. Perhaps these tales have travelled to the West through travellers, gypsies and missionaries.

There are a number of collections of folktales popular in Europe during the middle ages which indicate that their source is India: *The Fables of Bidpai*, *The Seven Wise Masters* and *Barlaam and Josaphat*. Joseph Jacobs, as early as 1912, made an in-depth study in this area and concluded that "a goodly number of the fables that pass under the name of Simian slave Aesop were derived from India," especially from Jatakas and Birth-Stories of Buddha. Besides Joseph Jacobs, there are a number of British scholars like Miss Freve, Miss Stokes and Mr. Campbell who published folktales in periodicals such as *The Indian Antiquary* and *The Orientalist*. All these scholars traced the origin of the folktales to India.

IV

There is a vast thematic variety in the texts of the folktales. These deal with gods, ghosts, fairies, phantoms, magic, superstitions and fantasies. However, these are not merely imaginary tales about unbelievable occurrences. The major source of the folktales is human society. A large number of tales deal with day-to-day happenings. Family relationships, marital love, parental affection, habits, love and fear find full depiction in these stories.

Folklore often reflects the religious, social and political picture of the olden times. The sociologists have taken a keen interest and paid special attention to the customs and beliefs of the people and the changes therein through the ages. The folklore is a reliable index to the life and background of the people of that time. If we make a comparative study of folklore in different parts of the country, we come to conclude that there is a common pattern in the writing and content of folktales. Over the centuries, these tales have been passed on from generation to generation verbally, by word of mouth, until they came to be systematically written and presented to the readers. The wandering minstrels and clan gurus have disseminated them.

It is noteworthy that folk literature is much more important in Northeast than other regions in India. This area, which is populated by a large number of tribes speaking different languages and dialects of the Tibetan-Burma family, exhibit a great diversity of culture, dress, custom and manners. Various ethnographic studies and books on tribal customs, myths and folklore have been instrumental in creating awareness for cultural diversity.

V

Folk songs or poems cannot be studied in isolation or bereft of social milieu. Such creations are the products of its times. They reflect the mood and spirit of the people. Literature or poetry is the product of the community; it offers the world-view of the community. Music or songs flow naturally out of such a world-view. To study the oral poetic tradition is to appreciate the origin of poetry and its significance in life.

In the world of music today, many music directors like Salim and Sulaiman Merchant have added Rajasthani folk music to their songs. They showcase a bouquet of Sufiana songs from the traditional repertoire as well as from Bollywood albums. Also they have performed to a rich folklore of several Punjabi and Sindhi Sufi saints. Conversely, the film industry and songs pose a definite threat to folklore.

There is a galaxy of typical folktales, a bulk of these are fairy tales, ghost stories, animal stories and stories of tricksters. One of the popular folktales, for example, is entitled "The Two Cheats." It begins in a typical fashion:

> Once upon a time there lived two cheats in a village. They were great friends. They soon found that they had been cheating the villagers around to such an extent and for so long that no one within ten miles of the village would believe them. They therefore decided to go on a long journey and find new victims to cheat.

The story goes on and further tells us how the two friends tried to cheat each other when they came across a booty. It ends on a happy note, with readers amply amused.

There are other interesting stories which hook the readers' minds and they find them unputdownable—like "Chhote and Mote," "The Prince and the Barber," "An Old Woman and the Hermit," "The Wife would not be Beaten" and "The Old Couple." The stories are so fascinating, told in simple and alluring style, that the readers are spellbound, willingly suspending their sense of disbelief.

VI

The tradition of narrating stories and listening to them comes naturally to Indians. "The objective of folktales in social and family life is entertainment as well as instruction," says Mahendra Mishra, a folklore specialist. Storytelling was common among the farmers, labourers and artisans to relieve the stress of their work. Even today, folktales are more popular in villages than big cities. These are all the same popular in the tribal communities.

The oral literature in India has had a great significance. This appealed a great deal to the social and religious segments of society. The folktales were largely related with various religious rites and routine family life. Religious traditions and thinking do not change frequently. Hence they have a lasting appeal. Today, these stories are amply available in written form and have found favour with the people. Mishra rightly quotes A.K. Ramanujan, the distinguished litterateur, who states: "Indian literature is as much written as it is oral. This is a *chakra* that is moving continuously. Oral is transformed into written and written is transformed into oral."

The narrative pattern of the folktales is often simple: the beginning, the middle and the end. The story begins with a statement or sometimes with a poser or from a question and its answer. A story may begin like this:

1. Let me tell you a story. . . .
   What about?
   It's the story of a magic boy.
2. Once upon a time there lived seven brothers and a sister.
3. Once there lived a great Raja, whose name was Salabhan, and he had a Queen by the name Lona. . . .
4. There was once a farmer who suffered much at the hands of a moneylender.
5. Once upon a time, when Brahmadatta was king of Benares, the Bodhisattva was born as son of his chief queen.

Such a statement is followed by the story and its progress. And finally the story ends, with a logical conclusion. The endings are like these:

1. And thus ends my tale.
2. The prince and the princess lived happily after that.
3. The prince succeeded to the throne, and ruled the country for many, many years in peace and happiness.
4. This is the moral of the story.
5. These are the ways of God.

VII

Folk literature is said to owe its birth in the universal desire to listen to stories. "Tell me a story," the child demands, especially when he goes to bed. Very often, mothers and grandmothers tell stories to their children, when pestered by children. These stories, seemingly simple and funny, convey their understanding of the world, their ideas and beliefs, their customs and festivals, and even about birds and animals.

The area of folklore offers ample scope in study and research. There are many areas of argument and conflict, and the researchers have many choices to make as per the requirement and interest. No wonder, important areas of research have been identified, namely, folklore discourse, ideology, folklore and ethnic identity, myth, magic and ritual practices. In order to fully investigate the area of folklore, there is a strong need to investigate the culture of a specification.

To understand the area of 'folk culture,' one needs to acquaint oneself with 'culture' as a whole. The term 'culture' in Indian context is *Sanskriti* which means refined, polished, cultivated. According to Supriti Phukan and Sarat K. Phukan, the term 'culture' encompasses the entirety of human activities in relation to its resources in cohesion with the physical environment. In short, culture is a sumtotal of life; it includes all the mental, psychological, social and physical means which make life run its course. In the present day, the story of cultural life of a community is done in the globe under various branches of knowledge: anthropology, sociology, history, geography and religion. Generally speaking, a historical investigation is confined to the origin, migration of the people; sociological study stresses upon the social life and its process of acculturation. In nutshell, culture is essentially related to society. There cannot be culture without society; neither there can be society without culture.

Folk stories have certain common features, viz., magic, miracles, supernatural, superstition, mystery and deception. The basic idea of magic is the belief in a vague, mysterious power which is beyond logical scrutiny. In primitive cultures, there was a strong belief in magical practices and rituals pertaining to magic. Before the advent of science *per se*, man was inclined to cling to his feelings and emotions. People in those times lived in two worlds—in their own mundane world which was material and visible and in the world of superhuman powers and the invisible. It was the belief in superstitions, supernatural and the otherworldliness which made them believe in magic too. It is said that the age of magic preceded the age of religion. Magic has often been associated with religion—both areas not having any rational or scientific foundations. As a matter of fact, scholars have established kinship between the two, branding magic as a pseudo science. In the olden times, the primitive man pinned up his faith in magic when his knowledge and skill failed. Folktales featured magic as an element that turned them mysterious and highly interesting. For all that is beyond the comprehension of man appeals to his intuitive mind. The storyteller employs various magical devices to astonish and amuse the readers.

Spirits play an indispensable role in the stories and plays of the traditional folk. A spiritual mention of the role and demons and witches needs to be mentioned. Even Shakespeare's plays, written in the sixteenth century, are replete with the doings of spirits, demons and witches. The witches are traditional wicked women who are expert in black magic. They negotiate with the devil and devour the innocent human beings. No wonder then that they have earned the wrath of humans for their ill-doings. They have been constantly persecuted throughout the world. In Europe, the witch cult survived until the eighteenth century, an era when reason and rationale dominated the society

A distinct feature of the Indian folktales is the use of miracle. Even in English literature, miracles and moralities have constituted a significant segment of academic curriculum. In Indian tales, gods, goddesses and fairies play an important role; they often help the poor and the miserable. They readily bestow blessings and give boons. Even demons are sometimes kind and come to the rescue of the helpless. Some tribal stories are noted for highlighting the sense of honour in people's dealings and their way of life.

Let us take up a typical tale. "A Funny Story" is a tale of a tribal village where an old Gond couple lived. They once had a quarrel over the food as each of them wanted to have larger share of the food. Then they made a compromise and set terms according to which whoever would speak first will have three of the seven *Bhakris* and the one who keeps silence will have four of these. They kept mum. Thus two days passed. No sound came from their house and the neighbours were surprised and worried at their silence. They approached them but each one of the two was silent. They thought they were dead. The story reaches its climax when the wife quietly said: "Alright, I will eat three, you can have four." As soon as the seven men heard her words, they thought the corpses had become ghosts and they wanted to eat seven men. In their terror, they threw the bodies and ran for their lives. This belief in the ghosts and supernatural was a common feature of several folktales. Stories such as this reflect the particular stage of the development as also the projection of the beliefs and fads of human mind. Rationality or scientific temperament is conspicuously absent in folktales, these being replete with superstitions and supernatural elements.

VIII

It is a pity that the present generation of grannies, especially in towns and cities, are not so well conversant with the traditional folk. The reason for this decline is more socio-economic than cultural. They are so engrossed in the day-to-day matters of existence that they do not find enough time to relate the tales. Villages in India, however, have not undergone such a drastic change. The inhabitants are still simple in an environment which has not changed much. This is in contrast to the people living in countryside in the West, who have adopted modern ways of life.

In the olden times, the supreme allegiance of Indians was not only to the political rulers but also to their country and the nation which embodied their spiritual-cultural values and aspirations. There was an intrinsic relationship between people and the surroundings. Ecology is therefore clearly linked with folklore of the nation. It is especially true of the areas in the valleys and mountains, lakes and rivers, trees and bushes. Inhabitants of these areas have a deep reverence for nature and mythologize it in their writings. "The formidable aspects of Nature," says Usha Bande in her illuminating book *Folk Traditions and Ecology*, "which the early man could not comprehend was responsible for the folk beliefs in animal and spirit worship, ghosts and demons, and other supernatural forces. Folklore thus is basic to their approach to life and their worldview."

This area of study and research is really vast. It has given rise to 'Folklore Ecology,' a science by itself that works between cosmic elements and life. It is not advisable to reject the folk wisdom as something primitive and insignificant. On the other hand, it is desirable that we pay due attention to it and relate it to the present, in our search and understanding of the universe and its phenomena. Ecology plays a significant role: it determines the condition of living and makes a deep impact on the pattern of thought and behaviour in a tribal society.

To elucidate it, one may take a couple of concepts, like the elements of water and fire. Varun is supposed to be the God of water. In Indian tradition and culture, Varun worship is one of the most important rituals of any religious performance. A significant ritual of marriage ceremony is Jal-Puja, performed on the day the marriage is to take place. This is known as Varun-Puja for the appeasement of the water god Varun. Often, the maternal uncle of the bride or bridegroom conducts this. In Punjab, it is called 'ghadoli bharna.' The relatives of the bride or bridegroom form a procession and visit temple, singing wedding songs, accompanied with musical instruments especially 'dholak.'

Like water, fire is also an object of veneration because it is a source of power. Several rituals of Hindu religion are clearly linked with fire, like 'havan.' A havan is performed on each auspicious occasion in the Hindu families, like inauguration of an event or business. Havan is supposed to purify our environment and render it conducive to better living and thinking. Fire also denotes fearlessness and bravery. We have 'Amar Jyoti' lit at India Gate, New Delhi, which stands for tribute to the Indian soldiers who lost their lives in the war.

IX

In the West, folk literature has been identified more often with America. The exaggeration and extravagance of American humour is said to have derived from the ingredients of folktales. The comic element is the hallmark of most of the American folktales. Many of the adept and artistic writers transformed meanings and subtle messages into mainstream folk literature.

There are a number of folktales popular in the United States today—"A Baker's Dozen," "Bear Lake Monster," "Adventure on the Rogue" and "Hoop Snakes." In Canada, we have "Crow Brings the Daylight" and "Blood Knife." Folk music has contributed significantly to the social and aesthetic culture of America. Many of the songs reflect the struggle, empowerment and perseverance of the African American community, thus embodying the struggle of marginalized people in America. Folk music is therefore important from a historical point of view as it offers a lively picture of Africans marching ahead in their fight for civil rights.

Dalit writings by Indians and folk literature produced by African writers have strong affinities. American folklore encompasses the folk traditions that have evolved on the North American continent since Europeans arrived there in the 16th century. Native American cultures are rich and diverse; they expound myths and legends that explain natural phenomenon—like how the earth was formed and where humans and other beings come from. Before the advent of printing machine, people were telling stories, reciting poetry and singing songs about their beliefs, dreams and experiences. Much of the material that formed part of American folk literature was passed by word of mouth from generation to generation.

While folk has been frequently used by American writers overall, it is in fact writers of African descent who have often resorted to folk myths and beliefs in their writings. The Harlem Renaissance from 1920 to 1940 was a period of the flowering of African American literature, notable writers being Langston Hughes and Zora Neale Hurston. The Harlem Renaissance marked a turning point in the history of African American literature as it is then that these writings came to be absorbed into American culture. Within a short time, it ignited interest in African folk and culture.

Zora Neale Hurston is the best known name in the area of black American folklore. She was a scholar of anthropology. She has therefore been regarded as one who sharpened her penetrating insights into the value and strengths of culture and its roots. With a great zeal and enthusiasm, she highlighted in her work "African presence" in African American fiction.

It is to be noted that folklore and Black Cultural Consciousness are closely knit. This is so because Black people share their past history to a much greater extent than do other Americans. As a result, it is their history, rather folklore, which has helped them to survive and sustain their culture.

Since Hurston was an anthropologist as well as a novelist, she could imbibe qualities of both the areas and blend them skillfully into her writings. This is equally true of Indian American novelist Amitav Ghosh who being an anthropologist could use his knowledge of the human history and geography to weave it in the body of his novels. Anthropology has given vast knowledge and analytic tools to produce quality fiction to both the novelists.

Hurston is a black feminist, whose work has ushered in a new period of female characters, reflecting the image of a 'new woman.' She is in many respects a literary forerunner to Toni

Morrison and Alice Walker. In the recent years, her work has drawn a great interest in India, especially in the way she has blended folklore with feminism resolutely and inextricably.

Hurston made a deep research seeking information regarding Voodoo rituals which she has mentioned in her books of folklore: *Mules and Men* and *Tell my Horse*. Her works throw a significant light on Voodooism: it is a religion of creation and life. It is primarily the worship of the sun, the water and other elements of nature. No wonder, Hurston has become a metaphor for the black women writers' search for tradition. Most of writers like Alice Walker, Gloria Naylor and Toni Morrison sought inspiration from Hurston for the spiritual kinship interest in such relations and the mystery of the world. It is admirable the way Hurston's works reflect a unique amalgam of folklore and fiction. She has sketched characters in her novels who are undeniably human; they serve as beacon lights for all those who 'ain't ne'er de light at all," says Alice Walker.

It is pertinent here to point out that African American culture shares many of its characteristics with that of aborigines in Australia and Maoris in New Zealand. Indigenous people in Australia are commonly known as the Aborigines. They descended from groups that existed in Australia and surrounding islands before the British colonization. It may be noted that in common parlance, the term "black" has often been used to refer to indigenous Australians since the British settlement. While originally related to skin colour, the term indicates the aboriginal heritage or culture and refers to any such people, regardless of their level of skin pigmentation.

The Maori and Metis in New Zealand are indigenous people who arrived there in several canoe voyages between 1250 and 1300. Over several centuries in isolation, the settlers developed a unique culture, with their own language and mythology. Traditional Maori culture has undergone a significant revival in the recent decades.

This is true of similar people in America, Canada and New Zealand. Primitive people in all these countries believe in a number of practices and ceremonies based on indigenous and oral traditions. They have great reverence for the land and other elements of Native. Aborigines, as also Africans, had developed unique instruments and folk styles. Adivasis in India too held similar views on their reverence for nature and other aspects of human life. Dalits bear some resemblance to the indigenous people in their attitude and bent of thinking. This subsequently led to the emergence of Jazz dance and music, and it branched into rock and roll, hip hop and reggae.

X

Interestingly, folk literature has contributed significantly to the modern Indian drama. During the 1970s and 1980s, Indian dramatists pondered over a vital question: How to draw upon various strands in the traditional theatre and revitalize Indian drama? Indian theatre started exploring indigenous folk forms which are different from Western theatrical expressions and much relevant to our times. The urge for a fresh outlook in theatre found wide expression in many languages including Bengali, Manipuri, Marathi, Guajarati, Kannada, Malayalam and Hindi. A number of talented dramatists looked for a new vocabulary, new styles and forms in their specific regions. This urge was mainly directed towards exploring the traditional and folk forms of our theatre or theatrical traditions with all its possibilities for imaginative productions.

Girish Karnad is among those Indian playwrights who rejected the imitative pursuit of the West and ventured into indigenous territory for their themes and techniques. He thought over the fact as to how the paraphernalia of folk theatre can become relevant in the modern context. Karnad says: "It was when I was focusing on the question of folk forms and the use of masks that my play *Hayavadana* suddenly began to take shape."

Hayavadana was published in 1972 and is inspired by the work of Thomas Mann entitled *The Transposed Heads*. The play is based on the idea that humans are imperfect and have number of limitations. Further, the play deals with women's emancipation. Padmini, the female protagonist, gives preference to her sexual desires and fulfilment. *Hayavadana* is the most successful example of the "theatre of roots" movement in India. This movement began after India gained independence from England in 1947, and the playwrights moved away from Western conventions in using regional languages and theatrical forms in their plays.

In *Hayavadana*, Karnad draws heavily upon the rich resources of the native folk theatre—Yakshagana, natak theatre and other folk forms with great deftness; it also makes use of the element of supernatural which plays a significant role here. The play employs the conventions of folktales and motifs of folk theatre like masks, curtains, mime, songs, the story-within-story facilitating mixture of the human and the non-human, to create a queer magical world. Karnad brings back poetry, music, a sense of gaiety and celebration associated with it.

Vijay Tendulkar, like Girish Karnad, is one of the pioneers of Indian drama creating exciting new moulds for modern Indian drama. With unique imagination and invention, he uses a variety of functionally effective theatre forms such as mime, dance, music and dialogue in verse, all invested with folk association. In his play *Ghashiram Kotwal*, he makes use of folk forms, modes of recitation and methods of narration specific to Maharashtra. His choice of the 'Tamasha' framework is particularly appropriate because it offers possibilities and sanctions for a non-realistic treatment of time and place, plot and character. The musical composition used in the play is derived from the 'Tamasha' and has a distinctive folk rhythm. The songs sung by the choral figures either comment on the action or help establish the appropriate mood. Tendulkar uses Marathi 'lavani' dance form to bring a sensuous and passionate element into his play and to highlight the important episodes.

The traditional function of the Sutradhar is to introduce the characters and initiate the events as well as comment on the action. Tendulkar enhances his role and allows the Sutradhar to narrate what happens during the time interval between Ghashiram's appointment as Kotwal and his ultimate exercise of power. Thus Tendulkar frees himself from composing the bridging scenes to fill up the gaps in the story. The continuous presence of Sutradhar on the stage also provides the necessary link between various episodes.

The Sutradhar leads the Ganesha Puja with which the play begins. Tendulkar makes him an active participant in the action of the play by making him adopt multiple roles. He plays the role of a passing Brahmin who is caught roaming on the road by Ghashiram. Again, it is on the Sutradhar's persistent probing that Nana's wedding plans are revealed. Later, when Ghashiram is thrown in the jail, he appears on stage as a fellow prisoner. At the end, the Sutradhar gives a running commentary on Ghashiram's final humiliation and punishment.

Since the Sutradhar frequently describes the setting, the stage is largely free of scenic display. As in folk theatre, the play uses very few stage properties. This enables the playwright to simultaneously present more than one locale. Thus the actors mime plucking flowers at one point, and act out the breaking of a prison door at another time. There is no visual break between these scenes. The actors do not leave the stage, nor do they move away from their earlier stage position. The play is thus an innovative experiment. The combination of historical plot and folk conventions add to the contemporary appeal of the play.

XI

"Once upon a time"—these are four familiar words that are filled with promise, leading into a world of fantasy and lore. We once sat by the side of our grandparents, or perhaps an indulgent aunt or uncle, to hear many a fantastic tale. This tradition is on wane with the emergence of nuclear families; children now are deprived of the togetherness and love of the elders. It is increasingly rare to hear stories being told in a time of packed schedules and technology-filled lives.

It is amazing that though the same stories are repeated over the centuries, the stories do not lose their charm. The secret is in the satisfaction that our basic curiosity finds in the folktales. Listening to them, we marvel at the mysteries of the world and especially many inexplicable phenomena of universe around us. Through the folktales, we seem to be widening our horizon of life.

Having said that, we conclude that folk literature has come to stay and is an important segment of contemporary literary and cultural studies. How do we account for the popularity of the tales? One can say without hesitation that both young and old have been enthralled by the lively recital of folktales. Their curiosity is amply aroused and satisfied by the incidents and contents of these tales. Every time a story is told, a new intimate experience leading to magical imagination gets unrolled. This is the whole essence and the sole reason for the existence of folktales.

The editors of this volume strongly believe that the folktales hold abundant charm for the readers. The present project is a modest attempt in that direction and if we succeed in doing so, we shall consider our labour amply rewarded.

Bibliography

Barman, Bhaskar Roy. *Folktales of Northeast India*. Delhi: Gnosis, 2008.

Beck, Brenda E.F., Peter J. Claus, Praphulladatta Goswami and Jawaharlal Handoo, ed. *Folktales of India*, University of Chicago Press, 1987.

Favourite Folktales of China, trans. John Minford, Intro by Zhong Jingwen, New World Press, Beijing, 1983

Phukan, Supriti and Sarat K. Phukan, *Onomastics in Folk Literature of Assam*. Guwahati: Students' Store, 2005.

Sen, Soumana, ed. *Tradition and Folklore in North-East India*. New Delhi: Uppal, 2000.

Sheorey, Indumati and P.C. Roy Chaudhury. *Folk Tales of Maharashtra*, New Delhi: Sterling, 1991.

Definition and Classification of Indian Folktales

SHUBHA TIWARI
A.P.S. University, Rewa
JAGJEET KOUR
Res. Sch., A.P.S. University, Rewa

In modern times oral storytelling has become a thing of past. Middle-aged people may remember oral stories being narrated to them by their grandparents. But today's generation, the millennial may not remember any such thing. All that they remember is watching Youtube and online videos. Oral storytelling was an integral part of life in good old times. It used to create and nurture a deep bond between grandparents and grandchildren. So many values, wise thoughts, *sanskaras* used to go down from one generation to another generation through oral storytelling.

The *Royal Institute Dictionary* (1999) gives definition of "Tales" as the "stories that are passed down orally for generations such as *Jataka Tales* and the *Tales of Aesop*." There are definitions of tales given by scholars, like King Attakorn (1976). They tell us that tales run through generations. They are passed down from parents to their children and grandchildren. These tales are an important part of our culture. They are part and parcel of our traditions. Most of the tale traditions are oral in nature. The basic nature of folktale is reflected through the spoken word. Now in the age of digitalization these tales have been written and preserved for posterity. The origin of tale is not very important. Everyone can take liberty with the storyline.

Folktales are flexible. In folktales details are less important, message is more important. The main aim of a tale is to entertain. They create an atmosphere which brings joy, enhances happiness and lessens the day-to-day burdens of life. The purpose of tales is to bring fun and enjoyment. The other aim of tales is to train young minds and set the standards of morality. Its moral function sometimes comes naturally. Sometimes it is added to the tale intentionally. Tales are not meant only for children. They are designed for the grown-ups as well. The tales of grown-ups are apt only for them.

Kulrab Millikamas (1975) said that the "Tales" are the stories that are oral. They are narrated by the people to provide entertainment. They are part of our traditions. They are our heritage literature. These are stories which help in strengthening faith in divinity. They are holy in nature and bring mankind closer to God. They serve various purposes such as giving moral lessons. They help us to develop better co-ordination with environment and laws of nature. The tales are stories which offer different moods and shades of human nature such as adventurous, jealous, comic, superhuman or supernatural. There are varieties of characters in folktales. Folktales have humans as characters. They also have supernatural characters. There are kings and queens, prince and princesses on one hand. On the other hand, there are common labourers, workers and housewives. Then there are ghosts, witches, angels, gnomes and mermaids. Each character is unique. The characters behave as per the setting of the story. They have their own code of conduct. A psychological study of the characters would be interesting. Sometimes they behave like ordinary human beings and yet sometimes they outperform themselves. They become extraordinary. Folktales reflect the atmosphere in which the narrator lives. Folktales also strike a common chord with the audience. In this way they are close both to the narrator and the audience. It becomes a cozy circle where emotions and passions are shared. The narrator and the audience become one. Folktales are all about erasing boundaries. They reflect all aspects of the human minds, its foolishness as well as its sharpness. Like a river flowing down the mountains, folktales splash humour, irony, joy, pain, challenges, ambition, anguish and suffering. Folktales become synonymous with life. The outer details may differ from region to region, culture to culture and faith to faith but the deep emotions are the same. Folktales tell us that all human beings are alike. The joys and sorrows of humanity are the same.

Sumamal Pongpaiboon (1997) pointed out that "Tale" is a Bali word and it means "story-telling." Folktales are strictly oral tales. The tales in written form share lot of commonness with the oral tales.

To put it simply, the tales are the proof of the human intellect. The tales are tools invented by the human brain to establish morality in the family and community. The stories are told by using power of word without using any material thing. The tales become a powerful medium to transmit values like brotherhood, kindness, honesty, compassion and love for nature. It is done in a very spontaneous manner. The tales are devices to put things in order, to maintain mental hygiene of a community and thus become part of oral traditions. The tales can serve variety of purposes depending on the demand of time and place. The tales are designed by common people called as folk. The tales which belong to common people are called folktales

Folktales are influenced by the specific culture. They are used to record events, important people and places. Folktales give information about religious rites and ceremonies of a particular region. They are entertaining and fictional. They embody fundamental teachings about human life and nature. They contain belief system by which people have lived for centuries. They are considered as formulaic narratives as they include traditional expressions and repetitions like seven sons, seven queens or seven fairies. They are simple as well as imaginative. All these things make folktales popular among children as well as grown-ups. The characters are imaginary with focus on action. Supernatural elements provide thrill and amusement. The folktales result in justice both for the good and the evil. The good is rewarded. The evil is punished. Most of the folktales are an effective lesson in the law of "karma." Many times a person is served with the same gloves with which he treats others. They teach wisdom. Folktales may be defined as short stories of unknown authorship which are transmitted orally for centuries and during their journey some of them are recorded in text form. Folktales are stories of people and they narrate how folks live and learn. Imaginative power of folks gives the stories better form and content.

According to William Bacsom: "Folktales are prose narratives which are regarded as fiction. They are not considered as dogma or history . . . although it is often said that they are told only for amusement but they have other important functions, as the class of moral folktale should have suggested. Folktales may be set in any time and any place, and in this sense they are almost timeless and placeless" (www.patheos.com/blogs/foxyfolklorist/folklorethursday-folktale). Indian folktales are both in verse and prose.

A.K. Ramanujan gives a unique definition of folktales in preface to his book *Folktales from India*: "a poetic text that carries some of its cultural context within it; it is also a travelling metaphor that finds a new meaning with each new telling." Folktales are fluid in nature. Ramanujan says that no selection can truly represent the multiple and changing lives of Indian tales. His definition of folktales does not limit the tales to oral or written forms. He frees the tales from oral and prosaic forms and presents them as our Indian folktales truly exist. He goes on to tell us that folktales are "literature of dialects of villages, street, kitchen, tribal hut and wayside teashop." They are common to rural folks. Folktales travel by themselves. They help in cultural exchange. They travel when they are told. Folktales cross linguistic boundaries when a bilingual person tells it or hears it. The structure of folktales does not change from teller to teller but cultural details get changed.

There are no watertight compartments or categories to classify folktales. Efforts are made by various scholars to classify and categorize folktales in various ways. Classification of folktales can be done on patterns, themes, content and purpose of tale telling. Folklorists have contributed a lot to define and classify the folktales. Indian folktales are unique. Their classification must be done accordingly. Indian folklorists have contributed a lot to classify Indian folktales.

A.K. Ramanujan is well-known as a poet, translator and humanist. He received the prestigious *Padma Shri* award from the Government of India in 1976. He inspired a generation of scholars in Indian literature, folklore and linguistics. Ramanujan was born in 1929 in Mysore city of Karnataka. Karnataka is a Kannada speaking state. He got his primary education in Mysore. He received B.A. and M.A. degree in English literature from the University of Mysore in 1949 and 1950 respectively. After 1950 he started his career as college lecturer. He taught at several colleges of south India.

In Belgaum, during his teaching career, he started collecting folktales from various resources. Any person like his mother, a teacher, school children, house maids, servants, aunts, men and women of his village who could tell him a story became his source. He continued collecting folktales until about 1970. His passion and interest for collecting folktales was extraordinary. Whenever he was invited to give lectures somewhere he used to collect the tales from school teachers, carpenters, tailors etc. He recorded the tales by using pen and paper as well as a tape recorder. Ramanujan, as we all know, is one of the celebrated Indian English poets. His poetry is known for its symbolism and imagery. He has dealt with highly philosophical concepts in his poems. He was awarded *Padma Shri* for his contribution to poetry.

Collecting and classifying folktales was his hidden love. Folktales always fascinated him. He never knew that posthumously his works on folktales would be considered seminal. In this sense his work on folktales is unintentional. Ramanujan read folktales extensively. He read *Tales of Grimm Brothers, Tales of Aesop, Panchatantra, Boccaccio, The Ocean of Story* (*Kathasaritsagara*) and tales that appeared in any children's magazine. In 1956 Ramanujan met Edwin Kirkland who worked in University of Florida and came to Mumbai. This meeting proved to be very important. Kirkland suggested to Ramanujan to translate the Kannada tales into English. Kirkland wanted them to be published in the United States. This recognition and appreciation motivated Ramanujan to study folklore at Indiana University, Chicago. Later he joined Department of South Asian languages and Civilizations as teaching faculty. He received his doctorate from Indiana University of Chicago in 1963. He taught there for thirty years. During this period his love for Indian folklore and folktales flourished.

Ramanujan studied folktales as a scholar. He wanted to clear the confusion and present a neat classification. Ramanujan considered folktales as a complete universe within themselves. He studied the structural aspects of folktales. He also studied the thematic aspects of folktales. He did a psychological and cultural patterning of folktales. It was Ramanujan's firm belief that folktales are not secondary to devotional or mainstream literature. He underlined the cultural importance of folktales. His classification, therefore, is unique and detailed. Ramanujan's classification is also important because it is a complete Indian point of view. India has a wide, complex and diverse culture. In maintaining traditional languages and customs from different regions, religions and groups, we need a clear understanding of folktales. Folktales have a very powerful influence over popular imagination. The heroes of folktales are worshipped in villages. Ramanujan was particular about the context of a tale. As we know, flavour is more important than accuracy. As the tales get retold in villages, streets, kitchens, tribal huts, wayside tea shops, market places and friendly chat rooms, they change colour. Most of the tales have rural setting and describe common people. Even the tales where queens and kings are involved, the masses have a strong role to play. There are many repetitions and similarities in folktales across the Indian subcontinent. Ramanujan says, "It is well known that such folklore items, like many other sorts of items in cultural exchange, are autotelic: that is, they travel by themselves without (often) any movement of populations. A proverb, a riddle, a joke, a story, a remedy, or a recipe travels every time it is told. It crosses linguistic boundaries any time a bilingual person tells it or hears it." The structure remains the same but cultural details change. (www.jstor.org/stable/1062747)

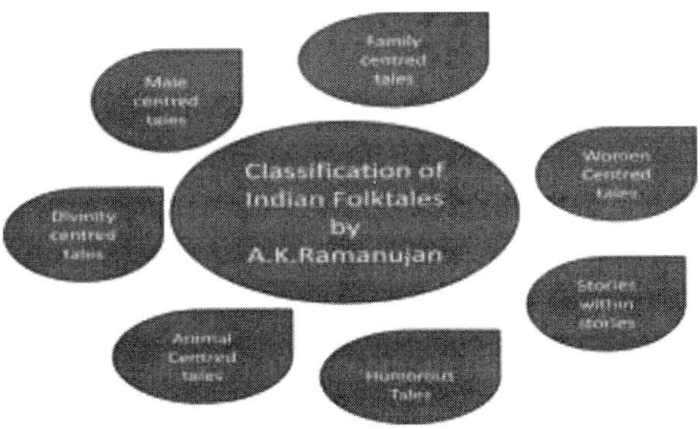

In male-centred tales, the male is the doer. A man usually leaves his native place in search of job or some hidden treasure or just to complete a responsibility. In the process he faces many challenges. He overcomes the problems and is successful in the end. He is rewarded by wealth. Often he is rewarded by a bride in the end. Many folktales end in marriage. "In *The Barber and the Brahman Demon* (Bengali), an idle barber does no work all day but sits in front of the mirror and preens. One day, scolded by his mother, he decides to leave home to try and amass some wealth.

In *A Musical Demon* (Tamil), a very poor Brahman grows sick of his poverty and sets out on a pilgrimage to the holy city of Kashi. In *Outwitting Fate* (Tamil), a young Brahman sets forth in search of a great sage who he hopes will impart knowledge. In *Winning a Princess* (Tulu), the youngest of three sons leaves home to try and win a princess who has thus far refused all suitors including his older brothers.

In these stories, the journey is long and hazardous, and the way is beset with perils in the form of wild animals or supernatural beings. While the men end up succeeding in their near-impossible missions, the women in these tales are typically just pawns or prizes or, at best, helpers." (scroll.in/article/801280/why-these-shape-shifting-indian-stories-need-to-be-read-all-over-again)

In women-centred tales, women outshine men. Women are shown as active, brave and intelligent. They often help men who are in trouble. In these tales roles are reversed, men are stupid and women are wise. One example is of the clever daughter-in-law who escapes tyranny of her mother-in-law and establishes her place in family. In another Kashmiri folktale named "The Wife who Refused to be Beaten" a young woman deftly tackles marital conflict by her wit and intelligence. She refuses to be ill-treated. These have control over the situation. They rescue males who are often stupid and weak.

Indian society has always been about family. Ramanujan says that a psychological reading of family-centred tales reveals Indian family structure, competition, love, hatred, cooperation, incest and betrayal within family. The family is the world. The setting is patriarchal; therefore a feminist reading is also imperative. In the end these tales are all about benevolence within family. The story of Savitri is relevant in this regard. As a young woman she goes out and finds her man Satyavan. She marries him against the stars. Finally she wins him back from the clutches of death, by her single-minded devotion and purity of heart. These tales are about siblings, parents, aunts, uncles and grandparents. The relations portrayed in these tales are vivid. They portray bonds of affection and care as well as rivalry and betrayal. These stories offer psychological insights on how families share love-hate relationships. Mothers, stepmothers, wives, fathers, stepfathers, husbands, brothers and sisters—all relations are interwoven with variety of human nature. These stories help us to understand the social system regarding practices of marriage and other beliefs as well. These family tales offer insight and understanding of conscious and sub-conscious human mind. The family tales offer stories of kings, queens and struggles inside their family to gain power or love.

In divinity-centred tales, magic, supernatural beings, forest spirits, demons, brahmarakshas, magical pots and plants provide awe and amusement. In these tales gods appear living and behaving like human beings. They perform all bodily functions. In these tales supernatural beings are defeated and befooled by ordinary humans. Indians have their theory of fate (bhagya) and human efforts (karma). Many of these stories tell us that a human cannot fight against fate but many tales affirm that we decide our own fate by hard work and effort. This reaffirms Indian philosophy of *Swa + bhava* (to each his own). Indian philosophy gives the individual the freedom to choose his/ her *Ishta* (god) according to his/ her nature, circumstances, time and place. We can also choose our theory of life. We find that in these tales depiction of gods and goddesses is raw. When these tales enter the realm of mythology, religion and history, they became polished and lose their wild colours. In folktales we find the characters close to life and even full of follies. For example the character of Bheemsen in the epic *Mahabharata* is different from Bheem of folktales. In folktales he is shown as a tribal. His wife Hidimba also belongs to tribal community. In many folktales he is said to have changed his rural appearance and disguised himself as a woman. So much so that in tribal groups of today's India the first salutation is Jai Bheem.

Ramanujan goes further into his classification with animal-centred tales. There is a huge treasure in the form of *Jataka Tales* and *Panchatantra* which humanize animals and pass on eternal values in an interesting manner. "The Monkey and the Crocodile," "The Tortoise and the Geese," "The Cave That Talked" are some popular examples.

Humorous tales make us laugh and enjoy the flavour of the story. Tenali Rama and Akbar Birbal are some of the well-known examples. Gopal Bhar was one of the nine gems of the court of Raja Krishna Chandra of medieval Bengal. Stories of Gopal Bhar are witty and comical. They amuse children.

We can also call them stories within stories. A fine story in this section says that a farmer had many interesting stories with him. But he did not share his stories with others. The stories got angry with him and left him. Stories must travel from place to place and time to time. Another story says that a woman was very lonely. She was full of the burden of untold stories about her troubled life. She grew fat and fat with stories. She had no one to share her stories with. One day she decided to tell her story to her favourite wall. She poured all the stories on the wall. The wall fell with the burden of stories. The lady felt light and happy. This is a deeply psychological tale. Untold stories cause misery, pain and heart-burn. Chatting, laughing and sharing stories are essential for healthy human life. Walls are broken when stories are told. These walls can be walls of self, identity, territory, languages, nationality, gender or class. (Mukherji)

Another important folklorist K.D. Upadhyaya has given another classification of Indian folktales. He founded Indian

Folk Culture Institute at Allahabad. The purpose of the institute was a systematic and scientific study of folklore. He wanted a coordinated study of different wings of folklore namely folktales, folk music, folk songs, folk dances and folk painting. Various scholars were working on the subject across India. Upadhyaya wanted to bring the contribution to one forum. The institute coordinated well with many Asian, European and American folklore institutes. Upadhyaya presented his work at Indiana University around 1963. (Dorson)

Religious tales have fructified from core religion. They may not be part of the Vedas and the Upanishads but they are popular among the masses. These stories educate people with a sense of authority. For example there is a story of two brothers Lord Ganesha and Lord Kartikeya. The two brothers enter into a competition where they run around the whole world. The one who completes the race first would be the winner. Kartikeya starts his journey on his vehicle peacock. Ganesha goes to his parents Lord Shiva and goddess Parvati, walks around them in a circle and sits. When Kartikeya comes after completing his journey, Ganesha says that he covered his world earlier. His parents are his world. This is how Ganesha wins the competition. This is religious folktale which imparts family values.

Jataka Kathas which are about the previous births of Buddha are examples of didactic folktales. Here the element of entertainment or *Rasa* is less. The element of giving a lesson and imparting a moral message is more important.

K.D. Upadhyaya has given a category to all great love folktales of India. Love has always been a strong motive of expression and literature in general. Saleem and Anarkali, Sohni and Mahiwal, Bajirao and Mastani, Prithvi Raj and Sanyukta, Shivaji and Saibai, Dhola and Maru, Mirza and Saahiba and Sassi-Punnu are some of the popular and important love folktales of India.

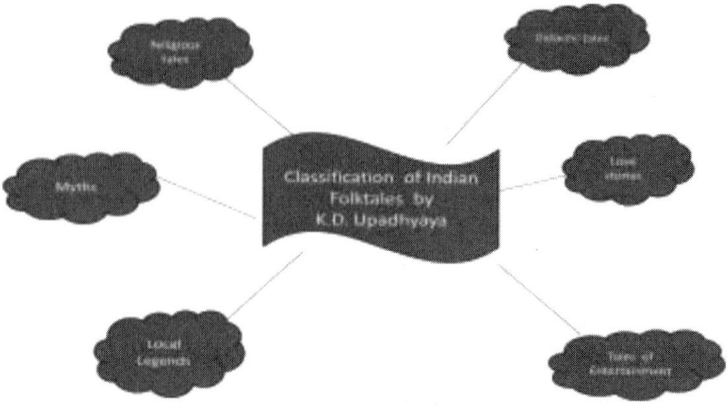

Certain folktales are created just for the sake of entertainment. These have no purpose other than giggling, tickling and connecting with the folks. In north east there is a folktale that a sage wanted to wake up to meditate but he fell asleep again and again. He got angry with himself and plucked his own eyelids. As the eyelids fell tea plants grew up. This is how tea became an invigorating and awakening drink.

India is a land of local legends. Every nook and corner has local heroes. For example Alha and Udal the two brave brothers are local legends of Bundelkhand and Baghelkhand. Pahalwan Gama, the fabled servant of Royal household and Ghag, Dak are local legends of northeast and surrounding areas.

The last category given by Upadhyaya is that of mythical folktales of India. This is where the boundary between folk and myth is merged. Vikram and Baital, Sulsa and Satuka and stories of various dreams of kings and queens constitute mythical folktales. The story of Savitri and Satyavan can also be clubbed in this group. (Upadhyaya 181-96)

We can see in modern India serious attempts have been made to understand and explain folktales. The simplicity of folktales has attracted scholars as well as common readers. Folktales do not demand much intellectual exercise and still convey the essence of living beautifully and simply. Preservation of the folktales of India is our responsibility. Stories grow our hearts. Folktales enhance our personality. We need to tell and retell these wonderful tales. They cover many aspects of life and provide simple solutions. The world of folktales is that of easing the senses and soothing the mind.

Works Cited

Bascom, William. "The Forms of Folklore: Prose Narratives," *Sacred Narrative: Readings in the Theory of Myth*, ed. Alan Dundes. Berkeley: University of California Press, 1984. 5-29.

www.patheos.com/blogs/foxyfolklorist/folklorethursday-folktale

Dorson, Richard M. "News and Notes on Asian Folklore," *Asian Folklore Studies*, vol. 22, 1963, pp. 367-81. www.jstor.org/stable/1177566.

Mukherjee, Oindrila. "A.K. Ramanujan's 'Folktales from India' could be the starting point for reading Indian fiction in 2016." https://scroll.in/article/801280/why-these-shape-shifting-indian-stories-need-to-be-read all-over-again

Ramanujan, A.K. "Where Mirrors are Windows: Toward an Anthology of Reflections," *History of Religions*, vol. 28, no. 3, 1989, pp. 187-216. www.jstor.org/stable/1062747

Upadhyaya, K.D. "A General Survey of Indian Folktales," *Midwest Folklore*, vol. 10, no. 4 1960, pp. 181-96. www.jstor.org/stable/4317882.

A Review of the History of Folklore Studies

M. SRILAKSHMI
D.V.R. & Dr. H.S. M.I.C. College of Tech., Kanchikacherla

The word 'folklore' was coined in 1846 by William John Thoms, the British antiquarian. In his letter to a journal titled *The Athenaeum* Thoms proposed that the word 'folklore' should be used in English to represent "the manners, customs, observances, superstitions, ballads, proverbs" and other materials "of the olden time." His letter was published in the August of 1846 and this good Anglo-Saxon compound word as mentioned by Thoms was accepted widely. This new word led to the establishment of an international discipline known as folklore, folklore studies or folkloristics.

The interest of scholars and intellectuals in the collection and study of the folklore materials has set the tone for folklore studies. Jacob Grimm (1785-1863) who extensively collected German folklore materials to explore the root German language became the most prominent activist in this field in the 19th century. He along with his brother Wilhelm Grimm (1786-1859) compiled some very important books, such as *Deutsche Mythologie* (a seminal collection of German myths), *Kinder-und Hausmarchen* (Children's and Household Tales, popularly known as Grimm's Fairy Tales) which influenced folklore materials in later times. The research of Jacob Grimm gave rise to a new theory named "mythological theory."

After Jacob Grimm, the first theoretical perspective in study and analysis of folklore was put forward by Friedrich Max Mueller (1823-1900), a profound German philologist, Indologist and a great Sanskrit scholar. He explained the meaning of myths and the process of myth-creation which strengthened the mythological school of folklore studies. He stated that Myths are created due to semantic changes in language where words used in the earlier times lose their original meanings in the later stages at the hands of the next generation. Though the Mythological school was abandoned later it is credited for being the first of its kind to attempt theoretical interpretation of folkloric forms such as myths.

By translating Indian anthology the *Panchatantra* into German language, Theodor Benfey (1809-1881), a German philologist and orientalist immensely helped in the theoretical and intellectual development of folklore studies. Benfey drew interesting similarities between Sanskrit tales of ancient India and the tales of Europe. He explained that such similarities existed not because of the genetic relationship of people as said by Max Mueller but because folktales travel across territories. He said that folktales emerged in India and later 'migrated' to Europe and other parts of the world through various means of cultural contacts between people.

The anthropological perspective in the study of folklore gained momentum due to the rise in anthropological scholarship in nineteenth and twentieth century England and America. Unlike the folklorists, the anthropologists study the material and non-material aspects of culture from functionalist viewpoints, and see the cultural norms and values as predictable and theorizable patterns of human behaviour. E.B. Tylor (1832-1917) and Andrew Lang (1844-1912) in England, Franz Boas (1858-1942), Ruth Benedict (1887-1948), M.J. Herskovits (1895-1963) in the Unites States intensively focused on this. According to this version the evolution of mankind followed a singular universal path of progress in every place, with three absolutely identical stages everywhere—savagery, barbarism and civilization.

Following Theodor Benfey's hypothesis, a novel technical method was initiated to study the origin and migration of folklore items. The Finnish national epic *Kalevala* was taken as a sample for this method which relied on the notion that though folklore forms undergo changes in form and content when they travel from place to place, they retain their basic features. This retention of the basic features helped not only in reconstructing the original form but also in tracing the route of migration. It was known as Finnish Method or Historical-geographical Method because of its research along historical and geographical scales. The major theorists of this method were Kaarle Krohn, C.W. Von Sydow, Archer Taylor, Stith Thompson and Axel Olrik.

Austrian psychologist Sigmund Freud (1856-1939) studied folklore materials and brought out books like *The Interpretation of Dreams* (1899), *Jokes and their Relation to the Unconscious* (1905) and *Totemand Taboo* (1913). According to his psychoanalytical theory, myths, dreams, jokes and tales are symbolic expressions of the unconscious human mind. He stated that dreams are the hidden reflections of the repressed desires of an individual in his or her subconscious mind whereas the myths are the symbolic expressions of the collective unconsciousness of a race or culture.

In 1930, American literary scholar Milman Parry compared the formulaic characteristics of classical epics the *Iliad* and the *Odyssey* to the Yugoslavoral poetry. His aim was to describe the form of oral poetry and to compare it with written verses. After Parry's death in 1935, his method was taken up by Albert B. Lord who published his book under the title *The Singer of Tales* in 1935. It was observed that the "epic singers memorize a set of formulas which enable them to carry on the traditional themes with reasonable accuracy and at the same time give them freedom to improvise new elements depending on the occasion without altering the form drastically" (Handoo 50). This oral-formulaic theory of Parry and Lord influenced in succeeding folklore scholarships, imparted useful perspectives on narrative composition of oral poetry and also initiated the trend in folklore studies to take folklore forms as more than texts.

Vladimir J. Propp (1895-1970) initiated structural analysis which considers any field or object of study as a system of interrelated parts. In his book, *Morfologia Skazki* in Russian language in 1928, Propp explained a new synchronic approach to the study of Russian folktales. He explained that the prime components of a folktale are not its characters but certain actions of the characters which remain constant in folktales of different regions. These constant actions result in similarities between different folktales. Claude Lévi-Strauss, an extraordinarily versatile French anthropologist, proposed another structuralist approach to explain myth, kinship and visual arts based on the concepts of Saussurian linguistics.

American scholars like Roger Abrahams, Dan Ben-Amos, Alan Dundes, Kenneth Goldstein and Robert Gorges began to take folklore items within multidimensional frameworks towards the end of twentieth century. In this contextual approach, the items of folklore began to be seen not merely as texts but as events, where the contexts of folk performances like storytelling, singing, rituals and festivals, and conversations were regarded as important as the texts.

Indian culture and civilization, unique of their kind, have been reflected in the form of oral and written traditions of the world. The *Vedas*, great epics like the *Ramayana* and the *Mahabharata*, the *Upanishads* and the *Puranas*, and bulky anthologies of folktales such as *Hitopadesa*, *Brihatkatha*, *Kathasaritsagara, Betal-Panchavimsatika*, *Jatakado* stand as true testimony to the vibrancy of oral and written traditions in India since ancient times. The works of Max Mueller and Theodore Benfey on Indian myths and folktales exemplify how Indian folklore resources aided in the theoretical development of folklore studies. Jawaharlal Handoo, one of the foremost scholars of folklore studies in India, has divided the growth of folklore studies in India into three periods: the Missionary Period, the Nationalistic Period and the Academic Period.

During the 19th century, language experts started understanding the *Vedas*, the *Upanishads*, the *Puranas,* the *Ramayana* and the *Mahabharata.* The British administrators, family members and Christian missionaries who propagated Christianity inevitably had to deal with local people. Therefore they learned regional language and collected folklore. By collecting folklore and mingling with the people, they understood the feelings of local folk. Important journals like journal of the *Royal Asiatic Society of Bengal* (1874), *Indian Antiquary* (1874), *Journal of the Anthropological Society of Bombay* (1886) published the folklore literature. The Christian missionaries started spreading Christian principles through their various folklore works which include Mary Frere's *Old Deccan Daysor Hindoo Fairy Legends Current in Southern India* (1886), A.J. Duboi's *Hindu Manners, Customs and Ceremonies* (1897), J. Hinton Knowels' *Dictionary of Kashmiri Proverbs and Sayings Explained and Illustrated from the Rich and Interesting Folk-Lore of the Valley* (1885) *and Folk-Tales of Kashmir* (1893), Aurel Stein's *Hatim's Tales* (1937), Charles E. Grover's *The Folk Songs of Southern India* (1894), John Lazarus' *A Dictionary of Tamil Proverbs* (1894). The British administrators and their family have published their folklore collection which include Flora Annie Steel's *Wide Awake Stories* (Tales from Punjab Told by the People) (1894); William C. Crooke's *Introduction to the Popular Religion and Folklore of Northern India* (1894) *and Natives of Northern India* (1907); S. Mahalinga Natesa Shastri's *Folklore in Southern India* (1884) and *Indian Folk-Tales* (1900); Robinson Edward Jewitt's *Tales and Poems of South India* (1885); George A. Grierson's *Linguistic Survey of India* (1903-1907); John F.A. McNair and Thomas Lambert Barlow's *Oral Traditions from Indus: Comprised to Tales to Which are Added Explanatory Notes*

(1908); E.M. Gordon's *Indian Folk-Tales Being Sidelight on the Village Life of Bilaspur, Central Provinces* (1908); Cecil Henry Bompa's *Folklore of the Santhal Parganas* (1909); James Tod's *Annals and Antiquities of Rajasthan* (1920) etc. These works of the missionaries and civil servants still serve as valuable references for folkloristic and anthropological researchers in India.

Towards the late nineteenth century, a sense of Indian nationalistic consciousness developed and Indian scholars and intellectuals began to search and established their cultural roots by exploring their own culture and tradition. Some of the major works of this period are: Lakshminath Bezbaruah's *Burhiait Sashu* (1911); Dinesh Chandra Sen's *Sati* (1917) and *The Folk Literature of Bengal* (1920); Zeverchand Meghani's *Halardan* (1928); *Dadajini Vato* (1933); *Lok Sahitya and Kankavati* (1947); *Suryakaran Pariks* and Narottam Swamy's *Dhola Marura Doha* (1947), Ramnaresh Tripathi's *Hamara Gram Sahitya* (1940); Devendra Satyarthi's *Bela Phule Adhi Rat* (1948), *Dhart Gatt Hai* (1948), *Dhire Baho Ganga* (1948) and many others. Many Indian creative writers and few western scholars also contributed heavily in the collection and study of Indian folklore during this time. One of the important works was of Verrier Elwin whose important books were *Songs of the Forest: The Folk Poetry of the Gonds* (1935), *Folktales of Mahakosal* (1944), *Folksongs of Maikal Hills, Folksongs of Chhattisgarh* (1946), *Myths of Middle India* (1949), *Tribal Myths of Orissa* (1954) *and Myths of the Tribal Frontier Agency* (1958).

After the Indian independence in 1947, the academic period of Indian folklore studies started which was featured with objectives of truth-finding, scientific analysis and preservation of Indian folklore by the Indians. In 1955, Gauhati University started the first department of Tribal Culture and Folklore Research. M.A., M.Phil. and Ph.D. courses in folklore studies were offered by many universities. Profulla Dutt Goswami, L.P. Vidyarthi,

K.D. Upadya, Kunja Biharidoss and D. Javare Gowda have undertaken research work in different universities and made folklore a subject for study. Some of the notable folklore scholars of this time are Birinchi Kumar Baruah, A.K. Ramanujan, Jawaharlal Handoo, Praphulla Datta Goswami and Birendranath Datta.

Works Cited

Handoo, Jawaharlal. *Folklore: An Introduction*. Mysore: Central Institute of Indian Languages, 1989.

Dorson, R.M., ed. *Folklore and Folklife: An Introduction*. Chicago: University of Chicago Press.1982.

Sahu, Nandini. *Folklore and the Alternative Modernities*, New Delhi: Authorspress, 2012.

http://www.egyankosh.ac.in/bitstream/123456789/48233/1/Block-1.pdf

Folklore Literature is Literature of Common Folk: A Reflection

PAVAN B. P.
Government First Grade College, Mudipu, Mangalore

Raymond Williams, a famous cultural materialist theorist and cultural critic, says that literature is a cultural agency to understand the history of that period. Folklore literature is not just about story or social rituals and it is one of the very important cultural apparatus in its own way. The folklore literature was mainly in the oral form but in the subsequent period it has became one of the important written academic exercises in the universities and higher education academies in the world. What is interesting about folk literature is that there is no one centredness or cohesive device and it is known for its diversity: it has fantasy, history, provinciality, narrative flexibility and more importantly freedom of expression and scope for dissent. The folklore includes local legends (Sthala-Purana), superstitions, proverbs, idioms, tales, and riddles. The Asian continent is a land of diversity in its languages and literatures, so folklore literature has contributed enormously to the development of the rich literature in this region especially in India. Even today most of the folklore literature has survived in the oral form in spite of the advent of the so-called print media. It has easily assimilated with the modern pop culture, cinema and popular music. In addition, it entertains both the literate and the non-literate.

When we look at the history of any country's literature, we find that the folklore literary elements are present in the formative stages of poetry, play, novel and short story. Womenfolk are the pioneers in the development of this art. They have developed interest towards folklore literature for various reasons: it might be to come out from their drudgery of work or boredom.

Let us analyze what William Wordsworth experienced in his famous ballad "Solitary Reaper." "Behold her single in the field, Yon solitary Highland Lass!" In the poem, the poet hears somebody humming a song at some faraway place. He doesn't know what exactly those words mean but he can grasp the meaning of those words intuitively. This is one of the best examples of how folklore literature can touch one's heart so easily.

Indian literature has umpteen folk stories and each story has its own device and technique to convey the meaning. The focal point in this paper is why we need folk literature and how it is different from other forms of literature. Invariably, folk influence is visible in prose, poetry, or play but its common elements make us look at ourselves and our societies in a witty way.

Two dominant features in folk literature are narration and history. These two completely deviate from the formal literature. In folk literature, history is not just documentation of the past events; more than that, it is a Sthala-Purana (legendary history/ regional narrative); it has flexibility and infinite possibility of imagination, native flavour, belief and, above all, trust. These Sthala-Puranas have been derived from great epic literature like the *Ramayana*, the *Mahabharata* and the *Tripitaka*, but folklore literature retains its originality and it adopts or contextualizes according to the regional belief and the faith of the people. To illustrate how Sthala-Purana has played dominant role in folk literature, two Sthala-Puranas of Karnataka are discussed here. There is a place called Muthathi or Muttatti on the banks of the Cauvery River in Mandya, Karnataka; it is surrounded by dense forest. According to local belief, during the period of exile, Rama, Sita and Laxmana visited this place. Sita lost her diamond nose ring in the river. Anjaneya/ Hanuman, an ardent follower of Rama, found the diamond in the water and handed it over to Sita by his gigantic tail; that's why this place is known as Muthathi. This folk story shows that even today people believe that Rama, Sita and Laxmana had visited this place.

Another rich folk story is related to Male Mahadeshwara hill in Hanur taluk, Chamarajanagara, Karnataka. There is an ancient Shaiva temple Sri Male Mahadeshwara. The Sthala-Purana or local folk narrative says that saint Mahadeshwara lived here during the 15th century; he had come to do penance and rode a tiger. Even today, Lord Sri Mahadeshwara's miracles are beautifully sung by the village folk artists in Janapada (folk style) called Kamsale. The epic story of Mahadeshwara describes the life and miracles of the saint. The broader structure of the epic resembles the *Ramayana*. The folk song associated with this Sthala-Purana shows the greatness of god. It is performed on Kartika Monday and Shivratri. The Kamsale is a folk art in which the professional singers praise Lord Mahadeshwara in their song; they use bronze cymbals for music. These professional singers belong to a particular community called Haalumatha Kuruba Gowda community. These folk songs have also percolated to modern Kannada cinema. The dance is acrobatic and needs a lot of dedication and is part of a deeksha or oath. In olden days, this art was only in oral form; most of the artists were illiterates. Though this folk literature borrows its main ideas from the *Ramayana*, it assimilates them locally with ease. One of the most hummable folk songs is "Chillidaru Malligeya Banasuryeri mele Andada Chendada Maykaara Maddevge, Chillidaru Malligeya," which praises Lord Mahadeshwara. In the folklore, there is local flavour, linguistic experiments and simplicity.

Folk literature has a paradoxical nature: on the one hand, it is realistic in nature, and on the other hand, it is rich in imagination. The stories are taken from common people and their day-to-day life. There is no concept of 'classic' in folk literature. Folk literature strongly believes in the suspension of disbelief and makes simple day-to-day experience grand.

Jataka stories played a vital role in spreading teachings of Buddha in an effective way. Buddhism was born in India and Buddha's teachings are simple in nature. According to Buddhism, there are four causes of suffering: Dukkha, Samudaya, Niroda (confinement) and Marga (Path). To escape these, Buddhism recommends Ashtangikamaraga or eightfold path which comprises 1. Right View 2. Right Intentions 3. Right Speech 4. Right Conduct 5. Right Livelihood 6. Right Efforts 7. Right Mindfulness 8. Right Consciousness. Buddhists believe that this eightfold path will liberate human beings from the suffering or Samsara (Life Cycle). However, it was difficult for common man to understand these teachings. They needed simple stories to convey the message in an effective way. Jataka stories were great help in interpreting philosophical matters. These consist of moral/ ethical stories, just like parables. This folk form was easy to understand for common people.

Let us take the Jataka story "The Mosquito and the Carpenter" to illustrate how folklore elements in it convey the message effectively. Once upon a time when Brahmadatta was ruling Benares, the Bodhisattva gained his livelihood as a trader. One day when the carpenter was doing his woodwork, a mosquito kept disturbing him. It repeatedly came near his head. The furious carpenter ordered his son to kill it. The foolish son picked up an axe and hit on his father's head. The mosquito flew away but the carpenter died instantly. Bodhisattva witnessed this and recited the story in verses in Pali. It gave the message that if we do something without right thinking, we will commit mistakes. This message can be part of Ashtangikamarga or eightfold path. The Jataka story simplifies metaphysical thought into simple moral theme.

Indian Writing in English and Folklore Literature have contributed enormously to the development of Indian regional literatures. In fact, folklore literature is a bridge between regional literatures and English writing. Here I would like to discuss two important Indian writers in English. In his first novel *Kanthapura*, Raja Rao introduced some folklore elements. These are: local dialect type of English, narration in Harikatha style and Sthala-Purana or legendary history. Though the novel is about Indian freedom movement and socio-political issues, he has infused folk elements very effectively.

Another gigantic literary bohemian is Attipati Krishnaswami Ramanujan, popularly known as A.K. Ramanujan. He was a poet, scholar, philologist, folklorist, translator and playwright. Besides contributing a lot to the folklore literature, he did extensive field research and collected stories from his mother, friends, relatives, servants and even villagers. He wrote these without any change of meaning in regional languages and himself translated them into English. Besides English, he was well-versed in many South Indian languages like Tamil (his mother tongue), Kannada, Telugu and Sanskrit. He also translated U.R. Anathamurthy's *Samskara*. Ramanujan's collection of folktales helped Girish Karnad to compose his famous mythological play *Nagamandala*. He took his stories from common people and made them extraordinary through his rich imaginative narration with a touch of regional flavour. His folklore writing was comprehensive and lucid in nature; it carried both instruction and pleasure. He proved that folk literature is not just for literature's sake, rather it is for life's sake. He infused the tempo of Indian life and Indian sensibility in his writing. Ramanujan collected folktales for twenty years, from 1950-1970, and confessed that he didn't know that one day it will be a great treasure of folk literature. His three notable works are: *Speaking of Shiva*; *Folktales from India: Oral Tales from India* and *Flowering Tree and Other Oral Tales from India*. He collected these stories, wrote notes and glossary for certain words and expressions. To maintain the effectiveness of the language, he used words like 'ayyo'—a cry of distress, 'che che'—no no; they are not just words but typical South Indian expressions.

Let us take a story from A.K. Ramanujan's famous collection of folktales *Flowering Tree and Other Oral Tales from India*. "Love of Kadabu" (Sweet Puffs) is a simple humorous story about a quarrel between husband and wife which ends happily. Once, a man went to his mother-in-law's house. There she cooked delicious Kadabu (staple food in South India, especially in Karnataka) for her son-in-law. However, due to certain formalities, he was not able to eat these to his heart's desire. To have more of these, he rushed towards his home. On the way, he memorized the word 'Kadabu' but forgot the word when he reached home. He said that he would like to have Badaku but the helpless wife was unable to understand what he meant. Soon, the verbal exchange turned into a serious quarrel and he beat her black and blue. Suddenly, a neighbour interfered and said that due to his beating, the wife's skin had turned into Kadabu shape. The man was elated to hear the word and told his wife that this was what he wanted to eat. He had forgotten the word but now he remembered it is not Badaku but "Kadabu." The story is full of fantasy, oral jokes and wordplay. Most of Ramanujan's folktales are not just stories; they are critical enquiry of human consciousness.

Works Cited

Abrams, M.H. *A Handbook of Literary Terms*. Singapore: Heinle, 1999.

Baral, Saranga Dhar. *The Verse and Vision of A.K. Ramajunan*. Delhi: Sarup, 2008.

Naik, M.K. *A History of Indian English Literature*. New Delhi: Sahitya Akademi, 1982.

Ramanujan A.K. *Flowering Tree and Other Oral Tales from India*. Berkeley: University of California Press, 1997.

Is it Magic?: Analysing the Gender Inequality in the Distribution of 'Mercy' in Fairy Tales across Cultures

SUDESHNA CHAKRAVORTY
Sushil Kar College, Kolkata

Traditional modes of expression such as fairy tales, legends, nursery rhymes and proverbs, to name but a few, are all part of a verbal folk art that for a long time has been giving durability and solidity to our understanding of the world. As S.P. Arya has discussed in *A Sociological Study of Folklore*, as part of the larger field of folklore, fairy tales have been used by generations of people as common philosophical guides, from childhood to old age. Being living artecrafts, these tales and legends may be in a process of continual change, but at the same time they provide a certain permanence to our whirlwind existence. And the academic world which has long woken up to the importance of the anthropomorphic study of the culture of any country, agrees that such study entails a thorough perusal of not only that country's written classics and literary masterpieces but its oral traditions as well, of which folklore is an important part.

This article tries to interrogate the extent to which the dominant patriarchal discourse about gender-appropriate behaviour in men and women is propagated (or negated) by popular fairy tales. My special focus is on how strictly this make-believe world of everlasting happiness treats its deviant or errant characters, and how the *gender* of such characters affects their fate and outcome.

As Ngaire Naffine has noted, the *official* version of Law, at least, is that it is an "impartial, neutral and objective system for resolving social conflict" (24). But in fairy tales from both India and the West, the mercy accorded to the women is starkly meagre in comparison to what is granted to its men. Far from being an impartial, neutral, and objective enterprise, law deals in ideology and discourse—in the meanings and assumptions embedded in the language it uses, in its ways of making sense of the world, and in its corresponding practices (see, e.g. Davies, *Delimiting the Law*; Hunt, *Explorations in Law and Society*; and V. Bell, *Interrogating Incest*). The concerns of Law, thus, often go beyond just making judgements on legal matters like culpability.

Feminist writers studying the role of gender in the operation of law have often found it either "sexist" (Sachs and Wilson) or "male" (MacKinnon 635-58). Carol Smart has argued in "The Woman of Legal Discourse" that law be approached as a "gendering practice," as "one of the systems (discourses) in society that is productive not only of gender difference, but quite specific forms of polarized difference (34). In other words, law is a "mechanism for *fixing* gender differences and constructing femininity and masculinity in oppositional modes" (34). This article attempts to show that the powerful tool of magic is unable to change the above workings of law even for fairy tale women. The law courts of today may have been the exotic courts/ castles of kings in fairy tales; but the justice, punishment and mercy meted out to the characters smacks equally of gender-bias in those tales.

While exploring the so-called "intersexual nature of violent crimes" in the United States, Robert M. O'Brien came to the conclusion that for women, "intersexual violence is associated with more serious forms of violence, but for men, intersexual violence is associated with less serious forms of violence." Further, he speculates that men "threaten women into compliance with minor assaults," and as long as women "comply," men "may not need to escalate violence." Women, on the other hand, will not be able to threaten men with 'minor' violence and hence may have to resort to major violence (151-70). O'Brien has argued that women who do not "comply" with and "submit" to men's demands spark off a "cycle of violence" and end up receiving "minor" violence. Women then end the cycle by resorting to "serious" violence (166-67) and men's responsibility for their own violence against women gets lost in a debris of comparative data, statistics, base models or simply the 'magic' of fairy tales. This is clearly illustrated in Giambattista Basile's seventeenth century Neapolitan version of the Sleeping-Beauty tale in *The Pentamerone*, 'Sun, Moon and Talia' (Tale 29) where the unequal distribution of mercy is even more blatant (Basile). Here, there is a king who, coming upon a sleeping beauty, rapes her (enjoys 'the fruits of love') and then abandons her. Nine months after this 'minor violence' on her, the young woman gives birth to twins. Basile's King is already married and his wife obviously is consumed with rage at the discovery of his dalliances with another woman. Her justified jealousy and sense of betrayal is exaggerated to murderous proportions and she is shown to develop ogre-ish tendencies. Blinded by jealousy, she orders the king's illegitimate children killed and directs her cook to prepare a hash of their flesh ("serious" violence). The story thus very conveniently shifts attention from the breach of faith committed by the man and blows the woman's rightful anger so monstrously out of proportion, as to convince all readers of her "innate" blood-thirstiness. The crime of the male is swept under the carpet as something understandable, if not actually justifiable!

In case it seems that I am putting the cart before the horse by applying such recent critiques to these ancient tales, I would like to point out that the very fact that the attitudes and worldviews prejudices reflected in these tales continue to dictate our life-styles even today, shows that public consciousness has kept these tales alive *because* they contain lessons which patriarchy wants to impart to its women (and men) *even today*, magic or no magic!

The fascination with a violent or cunning female offender is not really new. In the 1970s, for instance, a notion emerged that the women's movement had 'caused' a surge (largely imaginary) in serious crimes by women. But much earlier than that there were the fairy tales which showed deviant women and also the horrendous ends they came to, while the men committing similar or graver crimes often got away scot-free. Richard Collier has clarified, crime itself does not *necessarily* require strength, toughness, aggression or violence, but often the experience of being masculine is itself premised (or assumed to be premised) on the domination of women and children ('Masculinities' 293). These statements corroborate my hypothesis that the extreme lack of mercy shown to the errant woman in fairy tales is more because she has dared to step out of her marked space (of domesticity and self-effacing goodness) than as punishment for the actual 'crime' committed. In the traditional view, women are (or should be) nurturing, irrational, compliant, dependent, and incapable of strong critical thought. From here takes root the traditional claim that women who commit crimes are bad not as human beings, but because of *being women*. In contrast, traditionalists hold that men who commit crimes are strong and aggressive, as they *should* be. The only small problem is that in them these fundamentally *desirable* male tendencies are slightly exaggerated or unchecked.

The points made above form the theoretical underpinnings of my analysis of what the popular fairy tales depict, with extreme nonchalance, as the 'normal' way of regarding deviant behaviour. A case in point is the Grimms' tale 'Hans My Hedgehog' (KHM 108). Hans is the son of parents who were so desperate to have a child that they declared themselves prepared to accept a hedgehog for a son. Once Hans, the hedgehog son is actually born, however, he has to spend the first eight years of his life lying behind the store. "His father grew tired of him and thought: 'If only he'd die.' But he didn't die, he just lay there" (Zipes 156). In the next stage of his career, Hans finds himself in the woods, where he spends many a year tending swine and donkeys, but he also makes pacts with two different kings that result in promises to give Hans their daughters in marriage. The first king betrays Hans, but Hans gets even by kidnapping his daughter, then punishing and abandoning her: "When they had distanced themselves a bit from the city, *Hans My Hedgehog took off her clothes and stuck her with his quills until she was bloody*, and said: 'That's your reward for being false. Go away, I don't want you.' Then he made her go back home, *and she was disgraced forever*" (Zipes 157, my italics)

Thus, whereas one biological father's crime in wishing his own son dead is forgotten as the tale progresses, the woman has to go through a symbolic rape to atone for another father's (i.e. a man's) betrayal. The girl was being pushed into marriage with an unwanted partner and because she dares to let slip her discontent, patriarchy punishes her mentally and physically and she is 'disgraced forever.' The second king's daughter stays true to her father's promises, thus typifying the 'good' girl figure of the fairy tale. She weds Hans, thereby setting in motion the process that turns Hans from hedgehog into prince.

As Susan Edwards has pointed out in 'Provoking Her Own Demise: From Common Assault to Homicide,' there is a clear gender bias in determining what can or cannot be regarded as ample provocation for committing violence. Women are expected to put up with a far greater degree of provocation than men, which means that their actions are more likely to be defined as premeditated than seen as committed in self-defence or retaliation (152-68). It is this mindset which causes the revenge-seeking wronged first wife in Basile's Sleeping-Beauty-tale to be turned into a blood-thirsty ogre; while Hans' rape of the first king's daughter gets justified as having been done under provocation.

The number of stories in which the (male) heroes get away with not so moral acts, like thievery, conning of innocent people, or seizing power from the rightful owner, far outnumbers the few (very rare) tales in which such a street-smart protagonist is a female. Some such tales with amoral heroes are—'Tom Thumb' (KHM 37) (Grimm and Grimm 195-200), Perrault's master cat—'Puss in Boots' (Lang), 'The Thief and His Master' (KHM 68) (Grimm and Grimm 357-58), 'The Four Skillful Brothers' (KHM 129). In the last mentioned tale, for instance, one of the sons of a poor man becomes a master thief and joins his three gifted brothers to rescue a princess from a dragon. There is no hint of condemnation regarding the son's profession (Grimm and Grimm 603-8).

Tales such as the ones referred to above may be read as confidence-boosters for children, aimed at building character by giving the child the hope that even the meekest and weakest can succeed in life. What problematizes this apparently worthy endeavour of the fairy tales is its gender specificity. Amorality is condoned only in the man, but the woman has to conform always to the trappings of virtue, self-sacrifice, modesty and meekness.

The Russian tale, 'The Silver Saucer and Russet Apple' (Budberg and William-Ellis 78-84), for example, tells about three pretty sisters, of whom Aliona the youngest, is kind as well as beautiful. She gives a potato cake to an old woman who tells her to ask for a silver saucer and russet apple as gifts from her father. When these magical gifts arrive, the two older sisters start lusting after them. They take Aliona to the forest and in a jealous rage, kill and bury her. They then come back and ask the father for the coveted gifts. The father however, does not relent and with the old woman's help, Aliona is restored to life. The two wicked sisters are banished from their homeland forever—no second chance is given to them.

Undoubtedly, the two sisters err, because greed, jealousy, violence (even if we discount the act of murder as a typical fairy-tale exaggeration) can never be condoned. However the next tale that I will study, will bear out my point that for equally (or more serious) aberrations, the men are shown far more clemency in these tales.

In the German tale (not from the *Kinder-Und Hausmärchen*), 'The Tale of the Hard Heart' (Michael 58-67), we hear of Peter, the son of a charcoal-burner, who lives inside the Black Forest with his, now widowed, mother. Initially Peter takes up his father's profession, but very soon begins to feel discontented with his lot. One day, Peter remembers about the two magical figures—Dutch Michael and the Little Glass Man—about whom he had heard in childhood that they could make a person rich. Peter first seeks out the Glass Man, who though angry at the foolishness of Peter's wishes, still grants that he should be the best dancer at his inn, have more money in his pocket than another rich man in his inn—fat old Ezekiel. He also grants his wish to have the best and richest glassworks in the Black Forest.

But being foolish, Peter is not able to make profit from his Glassworks factory. And one day, when Ezekiel had a bad day at cards, Peter is consequently left penniless. Instead of realising his own lack of sense and intelligence, Peter places the blame on the Glass Man and decides to seek Dutch Michael's help next. Dutch Michael (a 'devil' prototype) promises to give riches galore to Peter if he gave Michael his heart with its capacity to feel, love, sympathise. Peter agrees to the bargain and happily comes back with money and a stone heart which performs the biological functions, but does not feel. Thus he begins to feel that his life had lost 'savour.' But Dutch Michael advises him to set up a house, a new business and take a wife—as this would dissolve all his melancholia. Peter acts accordingly and starts lending out money at high interest rates. No beggar ever gets anything at his door and he even refuses to help his own poor and old mother.

Lisbetta, the girl Peter marries, is good as well as pretty. She helps the poor on the sly and one day she is caught by her husband while giving some of his finest wine and bread to a poor old man who had collapsed under a great load of wood. Furious, he strikes Lisbetta with his cane and she drops to the ground. The old man, who is actually the Little Glass Man, also becomes livid at this and knocks Peter unconscious. Coming to, Peter looks for his wife, but cannot find her. His stony heart does not feel sorry for what he had done, and yet something feels amiss. Soon his wife begins to haunt his dreams, imploring him to get a warmer heart. After many such days, Peter seeks out the Glass Man and as his last wish asks for his original heart back. The Little Glass Man helps him to trick Dutch Michael and get it back again. His wife and mother—all forgiving—are restored to him and they return to a small but comfortable farm (gifted by the Glass Man) and live happily-ever-after. Thus, in this reworking of the Faust legend, unlike the original, the man is forgiven at the end and allowed to re-enter mainstream life, wiser and happier.

However, if on reading the above tale, one feels tempted to come to the conclusion that the endings are being softened and made more optimistic because these are fairy tales for *children*, one needs to only analyze another German tale, 'The Golden Duck' (Michael 1-11). It is quite a typical story about a widow, Mrs. Jutta who lived in a cottage in a forest with her daughter Adelheid and the two orphaned children of her dead brother—Heinrich and Emma.

Because they give shelter to an elderly woman during a dreadful thunderstorm, they are rewarded by her, who is, expectedly, a fairy. She is happy with the entire family, but benefits them by endowing a special gift on only Emma. Why Emma is the chosen one, is not clear in the story. The fairy's boon is that whenever she weeps, instead of tears, pearls shall fall from her eyes, and that the combings of her hair shall turn into threads of gold. But there is a condition—fresh air should never touch her face directly. Using this gift, Mrs. Jutta and her family soon grow prosperous, though this also led to a lot of jealousy among the neighbours, who even attributed these riches to Mrs. Jutta's alleged witchcraft. Meanwhile Heinrich, warned by his aunt never to disclose his sister's secret, arrives in the city to look for a house for the family, as they decide to sell off the present cottage to escape the hostile, jealous neighbours. In the city, Heinrich becomes friends with Count Wenzel of Hasenburg and one incautious evening, the count is told all about the beautiful and gifted sister, contrary to the aunt's warnings. Count Wenzel falls in love with the beauty described and wants to marry Emma, for her 'sweetness and loveliness,' not the gold or pearls, as money he had enough. "The idea of her niece becoming a rich young countess appealed greatly to Mrs. Jutta" (German Fairytales: Selected from Stories other than those by Brothers' Grimm 4). A coach was prepared so that Emma could make the journey shielded from fresh air. But owing to some incautious actions on the way, Emma becomes exposed to fresh air and transformed into a golden duck as a result, flies away. Left with no other option, the desperate Mrs. Jutta makes her own daughter Adelheid take Emma's place.

On reaching the city, the Count is disappointed, for Adelheid cannot, as per fairy tale conventions, be as beautiful as descriptions of Emma had set him up for. But he is ready to marry her, as a promise is a promise. After the ceremony, he realises that his wife is neither clever, nor bestowed with a sweet nature. He has a confrontation with Heinrich, who, having been kept away from Adelheid by his aunt, is unaware of the substitution and is very angry to hear his sister thus maligned. Owing to the fight, Heinrich is thrown into prison. One day, the golden duck (Emma) appears before her brother and recounts the entire story. The Count happens to hear it and now wishes to possess the duck at any cost. He had all but shut out Adelheid from his life and pining away for her husband, the poor scapegoat ultimately dies, leaving the coast clear, as it were, for Count Wenzel's remarriage. Mrs. Jutta is banished to an ancient fortress on the fringe of his possessions. After many machinations, the golden duck appears before them and transforms into the lovely Emma, who gladly rushes into the Count's arms. Thus we see that Heinrich's disobedience of his aunt and the Count's negligence of his wife go largely unpunished in the tale. But Mrs. Jutta's one act of desperation (the tale is very clear that she had been very happy at her niece's good fortune and that jealousy was never the cause of her actions) causes her to be banished 'forever.' And poor Adelheid, who is not even the 'wicked sister' in the tale, but merely a stop-gap whose consent for a hasty wedding is never solicited, has to die to clear the way.

Another tale that I want to analyze is from closer home—the Maithili tale 'The Infant Bridegroom' (Rakesh 86-94). A king is told by an astrologer that his infant son would die in six days if he was not married off by then. Once married, he would live as long as his wife did. To save his son, the king is completely unhesitant to spoil the life of an innocent girl. When his barber and priest report to him about a suitable princess of a neighbouring kingdom, the king dresses his minister's son as the groom who hides the baby prince in his dress. When the time comes for the bridegroom to put vermillion on the bride's forehead, the minister's son slides the hand of the infant prince out of his shirt and guides it in putting the vermillion (*sindoor*) on the unsuspecting bride's hair-parting. Thus, the woman is cheated into a life of celibacy and lonely suffering by the machinations of two men (This is a telling comment on our social conditions, where hapless girls were often married to men much younger or older than themselves for considerations of caste or cash). On the wedding night, the minister's son places the baby prince beside the sleeping princess and writing the whole story on the border of her sari, tiptoes out and rides back to his own kingdom leaving her to fend for herself. The princess, after recovering from her initial shock, accepts her fate without a murmur: "what is done cannot be undone. I shall live as the wife of this baby" (89). Taking as many gold coins as she could carry (her bride-money?) and tucking her baby-husband under her arm, she leaves her palace in the darkness of the night (for no fault of her own, the woman loses a roof over her head). I would like to mention here that the story records no attempts at a search for his son by the king who was initially so anxious about his well-being. Then begin her adventures, one of which involves her cutting off the head of her child-husband's teacher, because he lusted after her and her money. Thus, the woman is shown to preserve her 'honour' at all costs, suppressing all her natural and biological instincts. While the men are allowed to give in to their libidinal urges (cf. the king in Basile's 'Sleeping Beauty,' the prince in 'Rapunzel,' among many others), these folktales (or their editors) generally play the superego to its women making them behave as per prevalent social conventions, even though their world may seem to be fantastic and one that defies the logic of the real world. After a lot of twists and turns, the princess ends up with her now adolescent husband in the kingdom of her father-in-law. By one of the accidents so common in fairy tales, the minister's son sees the *sari* on which he had written his message years ago. Informed of this, the king gladly welcomes his son and daughter-in-law into the family fold. In the ensuing bliss, the original deception of the king and the minister's son are conveniently forgotten by the storyteller. It is the woman's lot to serve her husband and in-laws and make the best of things. What the two men had done in cold blood is not even seen as a crime, and so the question of forgiveness is easily side-stepped.

Fairy tales are usually told to children in the context of the family, and as Ramanujan points out, they are part of the child's psychological education. Psychologists such as Freud and Jung have attended mostly to myths; but folktales are also a potent source of psychoanalytic insights ('Introduction,' *Folktales from India* xxix). Childhood fantasies, which are part of what Freud called the 'id' and Lacan calls the 'imaginary order,' are made to accept the yoke of the 'super ego' or the 'symbolic order' through them. And that the socialization and acculturation process is inevitably tougher on the female (and how); is my contention in this essay. Maria Tatar writes: "Contrary to conventional wisdom, fairytale heroines have no monopoly on victimization. Male and female figures seem to suffer in equal parts, though the narrative duration of female suffering tends to be greater." (*The Hard Facts* 75)

But my reading of most fairytales shows that the man, even though guilty of major crimes, is rehabilitated, while the errant female is exterminated, whether it is 'Clever Elsie' (KHM 34) of the Grimms,' Agnisia of Polish lore or Sukhu of Dakshinaranjan's *Thakurmar Jhuli*.

Bluebeard's wifc almost lost her life for her curiosity about what lay behind the locked door. But when a male protagonist, for instance, Prince Ivan in the Russian tale, 'Marya Morevna,' also finds himself unable to restrain his curiosity about a forbidden chamber, he is not looked at with disfavour. "You must not look into the room that is bolted fast and sealed with tar," he is warned by his wife. "If you disobey me, you will bring misfortune upon us all" (Riordan 155) and yet that is exactly what he does and ends up earning more fame as a valiant giant-killer. The Indian tale that I want to use to illustrate this trend is even more interesting, since the very title 'The Adventures of a Disobedient Prince' celebrates the anti-establishment nature/ behaviour of the prince (Ramanujan, *A Flowering Tree* 5-15). In this story, the hero, the youngest of four princes, breaks all kinds of societal rules and familial protocol. At the very outset, he angers his father by declaring that he wants to do 'better' than him (6). He is banished to the jungle as a result. But in hindsight this only provides an excuse to allow him to have his great adventures, for when he returns to his father at the end of the tale, the father says, "If one has sons, one must have sons like you" (15). His disobedience continues throughout the tale, for when in the course of his travels he reaches the dwelling of a wise, but ugly, old woman (thankfully *not* a witch), he disobeys the one stricture she lays down—of not venturing northwards. Not only does he disobey her, but he behaves quite disgracefully even afterwards, taking away the clothes of a celestial woman, while she is bathing. In the first instance, the fairy tricks him and turns him into stone. But, unlike a Sukhu who never got a second chance, this prince is restored to life by the old woman. The prince is however not at all contrite, and repeats his teasing the next day. This time he is actually helped by the old woman (a potent reminder of how women often become tools in the hands of patriarchy), and the poor fairy is forced to marry this 'molester' in order to preserve her shame. So, for all his disgraceful behaviour, the prince is presented as the triumphant hero in the tale, who later on takes help from this wife to procure three more!

Folk- and fairy tales being a very potent source of knowing the people to whom they belong, the march of patriarchy carried out in them is too strong to be ignored. As I have mentioned earlier, feminist writers like Beauvoir and Millett have repeatedly stressed that since men always try to define women negatively (i.e. not as autonomous individuals, but in terms of how they appear to men), woman characters in works of fiction are actually the projections of male desires and fears. And this is true as much of the fairy tales (mostly considered as representatives of an oral tradition, though later heavily edited), as of literary works belonging to the written tradition.

Note: For a discussion on Lacan's concepts of Imaginary Order and Symbolic Order, see Fredric Jameson's article 'Imaginary and Symbolic in Lacan: Marxism, Psychoanalytic Criticism, and the Problem of the Subject,' *Yale French Studies*, No. 55/56, *Literature and Psychoanalysis. The Question of Reading: Otherwise.* Yale U P, 1977. 338-95.

Works Cited

Basile, Giambattista. *The Pentamerone*. Trans. N.M. Penzer. London: John Lane, 1932.

Budberg, Moura and Amabel, trans. & ed. William-Ellis. *Russian Fairy Tales*. London: Blackie, 1965.

Edwards, Susan S.M. "Provoking Her Own Demise: From Common Assault to Homicide," Jalna Hanmer and Mary Maynard, ed. *Women, Violence and Social Control*. Hampshire, U.K: Macmillan, 1987. 152-68.

Euripides. "Iphigenia in Aulis," *Orestes and Other Plays*. Baltimore: Penguin, 1972.

Grimm, Jacob and Wilhelm Grimm. *The Complete Fairy Tales*. 2nd edn. London: Wordsworth Editions, 2007.

Lang, Andrew, ed. 'Puss in Boots,' *The Blue Fairy Book*. 1889. New York: Dover, 1965.

MacKinnon, C. "Feminism, Marxism, Method and the State: Toward Feminist Jurisprudence." *Signs*, vol. 8, no. 4 (1983): 635-58.

Manu. *'Manava Dharma Shastra'* or *The Laws of Manu*, c. 1500 B.C. Trans. G. Buhler. N. Delhi: Cosmo, (1886), 2004.

Michael, Maurice and Pamela, comp. and trans. *German Fairytales: Selected from Stories other than those by Brothers' Grimm*. Bombay: Somaiya, 1969.

Midgley, Peter. Trans. *The Very Best of Grimm Fairy Tales for Special People*. N. Delhi: Book Palace, 2000.

Mitra-Majumdar, Dakshinaranjan. *Thakurmar Jhuli-Bengali Folktales*. Kolkata: Mitra-Ghosh, (1907), 2002.

Naffine, Ngaire. *Law and the Sexes: Explorations in Feminist Jurisprudence*. Sydney: Allen & Unwin, 1990.

O'Brien, Robert M. "Exploring the intersexual nature of violent crime." *Criminology*, 26 (1) (1988): 151-70.

R. Ford. "The Razor's Edge," *Boston Globe Magazine*, 24 May 1998: 22-28.

Rakesh, Ram Dayal, ed. *Folktales from Mithila*. New Delhi: Nirala, 1996.

Riordan, James. *Tales from Central Russia*. Harmondsworth, Middlesex: Kestrel Books, 1976.

Sachs, A. and J.H. Wilson. *Sexism and the Law: A Study of Male Beliefs and Legal Bias in Britain and the United States*. Oxford: Martin Robertson, 1978.

Smart, Carol. "The Woman of Legal Discourse," *Social and Legal Studies*, 1(1) (1992): 29-44.

Zipes, Jack. *The Complete Fairy Tales of the Brothers Grimm*. N. York: Bantam, 1987.

Shadow Plays in Karnataka

BASAVARAJ NAIKAR
Karnatak University, Dharwad

Shadow Play or Leather-Puppet Play originated in India and migrated to other countries of the world. "Hindu kings conquered Java in the first century A.D. and ruled for 1,500 years. During this long period of time Javanese life became Hinduized. Malay-Polynesian deities, which had counterparts in the Hindu pantheon, took on the corresponding Hindu names, and the shadow plays figures henceforth showed them dressed in the Indian *dhoti*. When there were no such Hindu counterparts for the Malay-Polynesian deities, these deities retained their Malay-Polynesian character and their shadow plays figures continued showing them dressed in the Malay-Polynesian *sarong*. In the course of time the number of shadow play figures was increased by the addition of characters taken from Hindu mythology" (Ulbricht, xv). This kind of folk theatre was prevalent in India even before the beginning of the Christian era. There are references to the Shadow Plays in Sanskrit as well as regional literatures. For example, in Kautilya's *Artha Shastra* and Vyasa's *Mahabharata* (1500 sloka). Harshavardhana's *Naisadha Charitre* (XVIII, 13) mentions that King Nala invited the Puppet-Players and arranged a puppet-show in the Hall of Entertainment (*Pramoda Bhavana*). Rajasekhara, a Kannada poet of 11th century, mentions in the fifth Act of his play *Bala Ramayana* that there was a puppet-player, who was playing the puppets of Sita and her maidservant Sindhurika and that Ravana mistook the puppet-Sita to be the real one and touched it only to be disappointed. Gunadhya's *Kathasaritsagara* of the 12th century mentions how Somaprabha, the daughter of Silparaja, presented her friend Kalyanasena with a box of puppets. Ratnakaravarni's *Bharatesa Vaibhava* points out the presence of puppet-players among the visitors to Emperor Bharata's court. There are references to the Shadow Play in the *vachanas* of *saranas*, who lived in the twelfth century Karnataka and in the *kirtanas* of Kanakadasa in sixteenth century Karnataka. Cennabasava, one of such *saranas*, makes a reference to the Shadow Plays in one of his *vachanas*. Kaliketa Bommayya, another *sarana* of the same galaxy, is said to have been a *killiketa* i.e. professional shadow-play artist.

There was a *virakta* called Santa, the puppet-player (Gombeyadisuva kayakada Santa) during the reign of Emperor Srikrisnadevaraya (1419-1446). Kanakadasa, one of the famous Haridasas of the same period refers to the puppet-play by saying that the whole cosmos is engaged in a puppet-play.

There is a reference to Kalaketa in *Basava Purana*, which is interpreted variously by different scholars. Dr. L. Basavaraju (in his Preface to *Sivadasa Gitanjali*, 38) opines that the Kalaketa Bommayya used to entertain the devotees by performing the role of Virabhadra and conduct the *dasoha* out of the money collected through his *kayaka*. But there is no clear reference to any Shadow Play here. There are references to Shadow Plays in Dhanapala's *Tilaka Manjari*, Vidyaranya's *Pancadasi*, Palkurike Somanath's *Panditaradhya's Carita* and the *kirtanas* of Kanakadasa and Purandaradasa. The Shadow Theatre enjoyed royal patronage during the reign of Rastrakutas, Kadambas, Chalukyas and Hoysalas, especially that of Vijayanagara Emperors.

The Indians believe in the divine origin of all arts. In spite of such romantic belief by people in general, the scholars have continued to debate whether the Shadow Play preceded the

Puppet Play or vice versa or whether the puppet theatre preceded the human theatre.

Shadow Play is one of the best forms of folk art. Being a professional art, it has employed all the techniques of attracting the popular attention. One may notice a sort of evolution in the history of this art. Broadly speaking, two phases can be deciphered in its evolution. In the first phase, the transparent and figural cutouts were employed. Then as years went by, the cutout puppets were made to move their limbs like hands and legs. Later the theme, technique and music of *Yakshagana* were incorporated into the shadow play. In the second phase, the shadow play was based on ballads (*lavanis*) and epics like the *Ramayana* and the *Mahabharata*. Both the forms of shadow play are luckily prevalent in Karnataka, although it is difficult to decide which of them preceded the other. Whether one form was the logical consequence of the other or whether both of them grew simultaneously or independently are yet to be researched into.

The picturesqueness and multicoloured nature of the Shadow Play helps us to establish some connection between the folk-paintings, which preceded this theatre. For example, in ancient India, people had the habit of getting the walls of caves and temples painted; or getting woven picturesque clothes and gifting them away to temples; or getting the pictures of favourite gods painted on wooden boards. Similarly, they had the habit of getting a series of pictures connected with a single theme drawn or painted on a roll of cloth and exhibiting them to the public on proper occasions. Such practice could be seen in Vedic, Jain and Buddhist traditions. Chilvin Norris, a French scholar opines that *'Patakatha'* or 'Canvas Story' is older than the Sanskrit drama. A Jain *Purana* entitled *Kuvalayamala* mentions that a Jain monk used to offer his religious discourses with the help of a roll of pictures. Similarly there are references to *'Patacitra'* or 'Canvas

Picture' in Buddhist literature and to *'Yama Pata'* in Sanskrit *Puranas*.

The Jain volume of palm leaves entitled *Mahadhavala* is modelled after the folk painting and drawing. There are references to *'citrapata'* (canvas of pictures) in the Old Kannada prose work, *Vaddaradhane* by Sivakotyacarya and Pampa's *Adipurana*. In the *Mahabharata* there has been a tradition for centuries of entertaining people during the Navaratri festival with the help of a canvas of pictures and to the accompaniment of *Bhagavata-Vina*. The nomadic community of Rajasthan called *'Thakurs'* cultivated this art as a hereditary one. The *'Garoda'* people of Gujarat employ a scroll of pictures called *'Bapuji ki Padacitra saruli'* to propagate the heroism of their kings and the greatness of the Jain *tirthankaras*. Similarly the roll of pictures measuring three feet in width and thirty feet in length are said to be available in Bengal, Bihar, Orissa and Andhra Pradesh (especially Telangana area).

The directors of leather-puppet plays are called *'killiketas'* in Belgaum, Dharwad, Bijapur and Bellary districts and *'katabas'* in Gulbarga district and *'Gomberamas'* or *'Chitra Marutis'* in old Mysore area. They are also called by different names like *Sillekyata, Katabujata, Kolukyata, Astrikyata, Kalikyata, Bundekyata*, etc. The members of *killiketa* community are the professional artists of this folk-theatre. The meaning of the word *'killiketas'* is interpreted variously. Some scholars guess that it must have been directed from *'kilu katha'* (vulgar story). The artists, who must be narrating low or vulgar stories originally must have later come under the influence of *Yakshagana Bayalatas* and taken to the narration of stories from the *Ramayana* and the *Mahabharata*. H.K. Ranganath has illustrated this in his *The Karnataka Theatre*. The Puppet-Theatre is known by different names in different geographical locations of India. It is called *Kathputli* in Hindi, *Kalasutri Bihayi* in Marathi (Maharashtra), *Tolu Bommalata* in Telugu (Andhra Pradesh)

Killikyatara Ata, Gombi Ata and *Gomberamara Ata* in Kannada (Old Mysore), *Katabara Ata* in Bijapur and Gulbarga districts and as *Mandyana* Ata in some parts of Karnataka.

A correct historical picture of the tradition of Shadow Play is available in the *Gazetteer of Bombay* (Vol. XXIII) prepared in 1884, which contains some solid information about *killiketas* (196-201). According to it, *killiketas* were also called *katabas* and the ancestor of *killiketas* was a *kshatriya*, who accompanied the Pandavas during the latter's exile. According to Edgar Thurston, "The *Killiketas* are a Marathi-speaking people, who amuse villagers with their marionette shows in the Telugu and Canarese countries" (293). As S.M. Natesa Sastri says, "Their profession is enacting religious dramas before the village public (whence their name, meaning buffoon). The black *kambli* (blanket) is their screen, and any *mandapa* or village *chavadi*, or open house is their stage. Night is the time for giving the performance. They carry with them pictures painted in colours on deer skins, which are well-tanned, and made fine like parchment. The several parts of the picture representing the human or animal body are attached to each other by iron wires, and the parts are made to move by the assistance of thin bamboo splits, and thus the several actions and emotions are represented to the public, to the accompaniment of songs. Their pictures are in most cases very fairly painted, with variety and choice of colours. The stories chosen for representation are generally from the *Ramayana* and the *Mahabharata*, which they call *Ravanyakatha* and *Pandavakatha*—the stories of Ravana and the Pandavas" (*Indian Review*, VII, 1906, qtd. Thurson 293). Thurston further says that the dead of these *killikyatas* are buried in a seated posture and that some of their women are engaged as professional tattoers.

All the *killiketas* know Kannada and have no traditional story to prove that they migrated to Karnataka from Andhra Pradesh. It, therefore, means that they had settled down in

Karnataka for long. They use a mixture of Kannada and Marathi at home. They follow a rule of their community that they must tour the country at least once in three months. However, if they cannot tour, they are expected at least to change their oven in the kitchen from one place to another. The men-folk go for fishing during the daytime, but perform the Shadow Play during the night. These *killiketas* possess lands in Bagilukote, Badami, Hunagund and other places, gifted to them in the past. But they do not cultivate them by themselves. After the introduction of the Law of disarmament and Prohibition against Deforestation, the people of these areas invite and hire the *killiketas* to kill the pigs, which ruin the crops in the fields. The *killiketas* have many sub-sects among them, decided by their specific professions. They follow many rituals ranging from birth to death.

An important piece of information given in the *Bombay Gazetteer* is a *sannad* dated Fasali Year 930 (1520 or 1521) given to the *killiketas* by the Second Sultan of Bijapur. Ismail, the Second Sultan of Adilshahi family of Bijapur, ruled from 1510 to 1534. These historical facts prove that the Shadow Plays used to be performed by *killiketas* by 1520. Since they had land grants, they must have had good social status also. The *Gazetteer* mentions that there was no change in the life-style for the past two or three centuries. This takes their ancestry still further back.

The *Gazetteer* of Belgaum published by the Old Bombay State mentions that *killiketas* have migrated in groups from Kolhapur and Satara of Maharashtra to Karnataka. (196) The *Gazetteer* of Bijapur district mentions that their domestic language was Marathi with a mixture of Kannada.

The *Mysore Castes and Tribes* (513-35) offers detailed information about the *killiketas*. It says that the *killiketas* used to get land grants from the rulers for their entertaining service. The book also refers to an interesting story about the ancestor of *killiketas*. The *killiketas* were originally the agriculturists of Maharashtra. One of their women had an illegal relation with a goldsmith called Kattare Kalachari. Even after the adultery was publicly known, she lived with him and bore him seven sons. Consequently she was excommunicated and did not know how to earn her livelihood. The lover Kalachari taught her the art of cutting the leather-puppets, singing and entertaining through which she could earn her livelihood. Thus they formed a caste of their own, joined in by their relatives also. Later they migrated group by group to the southern parts of the country like Karnataka.

Though one may guess the ancestry of the Shadow Play with the help of the word *'killiketas'* and their autobiographical information, one cannot fix a cutout date for its ancestry. Some scholars opine that there is evidence to prove that the Shadow Theatre was prevalent in Andhra Pradesh as early as the third century B.C. It had reached its height during the reign of Satavahana, Pallava, Chalukya, Kakatiya dynasties and during the reign of the Kings of Vijayanagara and Tanjavuru. It travelled to South East Asia along with the Indians, who migrated to those places through the coastal cities like Kalinga, Jeemani, Korangi and Vadre. But there can be another method of deciding its ancestry by comparing it with similar art found in Siam, Indo-China, Jawa and Bali. Though such plays are performed in these countries by Muslims, the themes happen to be Indian. This theatre must have gone there at some point of time when they were ruled by the Emperors of South India. A Chola King bearing the title 'Gangaikonda' (perhaps Rajarajendra Chola, 1012-44) is said to have ruled over these countries when the Shadow Theatre migrated there.

Some scholars conjecture that the Shadow Theatre must have migrated from the coast of Andhra Pradesh to Southeast Asia; that the Arabs must have taken it from Jawa to Arabia; and that it must have migrated from Arabia to Syria, Turkey and North Africa. They further opine that the ancient Indian saints and philosophers must have used the Shadow Plays for the propagation of religion and moral edification. Though this art developed into a means of entertainment later, it never gave up its basic didactic purpose. (Shyam Parmar, *Traditional Folk Media in India*, 1975).

For the preparation of the leather puppet-stage, the puppeteer requires four bamboo poles for fixing in the earth at four corners and four bamboo poles for connecting them at the top corners. The three sides, except the front and top, are covered with a mat or with coconut fronds. Then a black blanket and a white *dhoti* are required for the performance of leather puppets. The stage is decorated with mango leaves, a sign of auspiciousness.

The stage required for the performance of small leather-puppets by the puppeteer in a sitting position is generally of six feet in height and eight feet square. The front position of the stage is fixed with an immaculately white *dhoti* of three and a half feet width for a curtain. Below the *dhoti*, a black blanket of one and a half feet width is fixed.

The puppeteers sit inside the stage behind the black blanket, but they are not visible to the audience on account of the black curtain. A wick lamp or electric lamp is hung behind the puppeteers. When they hold the leather-puppets between the lamp and the white curtain, the puppets cast wonderful multi-coloured shadows on the white curtain thereby creating a magical world for the audience. Most of the puppeteers including singers, instrumentalists and helpers belong to the same caste of *killiketas* and to the same family.

But the stage required for the performance of life-size or bigger than life-size puppets is quite different from that of small puppets and resembles almost the stage of folk-theatre (*bayalata*). Whether the puppets are big or small, the puppeteer has to be an expert in handling the leather-puppets very dexterously. On the whole, the performance of small leather-puppets is said to be far more attractive than that of big ones.

Such performances are sure to capture the attention of folk audiences.

The location for the performance of the leather-puppets may be any convenient place. Referring to *killiketas* and their performances, S.M. Natesh Shastry says, "Their profession is enacting religious dramas before the village public. The black *kambali* is their screen, and any *mandapa* or village *chavadi* or open house is their stage. They carry with them pictures painted in colours and deer skins, which are well-tanned and made fine like parchments" (*Indian Review*, VIII, 1906). He has also referred to the way in which the different parts of the pictures are joined with thin wire and how the parts are made to move with the help of very thin sticks, how they exhibit their dexterity in controlling the puppets, how their singing was accompanied by instrumental music and how the themes were borrowed from epics like the *Ramayana* and the *Mahabharata.*

The maximum duration of a leather-puppet or shadow play is of three hours. The puppeteer camps in a village for about a fortnight along with his troupe. From the first day of his camp, the people of different lanes of the village invite him (by offering him *vilya*) to perform the thematic events of their choice in the next few days. Thus both the puppeteer and the villagers schedule the calendar of performances carefully and see that there is no repetition of themes in that village. In fixing the dates of shows, both the parties take care to see that the series of performances follow some chronological order or a principle of thematic continuity. For example, the first show in a village depicts the theme of Kauravas poisoning Bhima; the second show would depict the chess play between Kauravas and Pandavas. The next show would depict the exile of Pandavas. The next show would depict the killing of the demon Kamsa and the last one would depict the war of Kurukshetra. Thus all these shows put together would offer an overview of the *Mahabharata*. Mr. Keshappa of Kakanur village of Badami *taluka* of Bagalkot district has the ability to present the main episodes of the *Mahabharata* in twenty-one shows on twenty-one nights. Each play has a patch of humour for about fifteen to twenty minutes for the entertainment of people.

The number of camping days may range from fifteen to thirty days or even to a couple of months in different villages. On the last day the puppeteer offers a free show in front of the village temple, as a mark of gratitude to his patrons, who have paid him in cash or kind for so many days. The next day he would leave the village along with his troupe for the next village.

The main substance with which the leather-puppets are made is the animal hide, especially that of deer or goat. But the general opinion of these artists is that deerskin is best suited to this purpose on account of its transparency and durability. But in the border area between Karnataka and Andhra Pradesh, even buffalo-hide is used for the preparation of life-size puppets.

The leather-puppeteers used to get the deer skin mainly by hunting the animals. Sometimes the *gowdas* i.e. village chiefs used to hunt the animals and donate their hides to puppeteers and ask them to prepare the puppets in memory of their (donors') ancestors. Sometimes they used to buy the animal hides and donate them to the puppeteers.

After acquiring the animal hide, the puppeteer has to take the responsibility of seasoning it, cutting it into required shapes and sizes and painting them appropriately. He has to follow a very careful method of seasoning the animal hide in order to make it transparent as well as durable. He would first soak the hide in water, then scrape off the hairs and sundry it. Now the hide looks like a transparent paper or glass. Then he would carve the outline of the required picture on it with a sharp bodkin-like instrument and cut it off separately.

There are two types of leather-puppets: one, comprehensive puppets containing the figures of man, chariot, charioteer and weapons; two, individual puppets whose hands, trunks, legs and hands are prepared separately and joined together to facilitate the easy movement of limbs.

Whether the puppets are comprehensive or individual, the method of preparing them is the same. The puppeteer has to carve the outlines very carefully and pierce tiny or relatively big holes to create the impression of ornaments (including even crests).

The next stage is of painting the puppets. The paints are also prepared by the puppeteers themselves. In the earlier days, such paints were prepared out of roots, leaves, barks and fruits of trees. But later, paints had to be bought from shops. The puppeteers have to select only the prominent and durable colours, which are bewitching to the eyes. The colours like red, black and yellow are used prominently. Though such colours painted on the leather-puppets may look rather dull, they look very attractive when they are held against the light. The painted puppets are dried in shade and never in sunlight lest the colour should fade.

In the earlier days, the entire puppets used to be sewed to small bamboo sticks with the help of which the puppeteers used to play them. Here the entire puppets were to dance. The movement of limbs was not possible. But later more flexibility was introduced into the preparation of leather-puppets. Three parts of the body like neck; chest and waist are sewn to a bamboo stick to make them look erect. Then head, hands, thighs and legs are sewn with a string separately thereby facilitating their movement. If the puppets are small, the puppeteer has to sit behind the curtain and perform the play. If the puppets are of life-size, then he has to stand upright to perform the play. The time when such flexible puppets came into existence is not known precisely. But it seems possible that there was some influence of string-puppets upon them.

The neat preservation of these leather-puppets is also an art. The puppeteer has to see that the puppets do not grow dry or brittle. He has, therefore, to apply some kind of liquid prepared by him out of roots and leaves. If properly preserved like this, the leather-puppets last for more than hundred years. After the performance is over, the puppeteer keeps the puppets neatly arranged in a bamboo box called *'bavali,'* which is held in high reverence by him.

The preparation of new leather-puppets is not an easy task. First of all it is a very costly affair and the artists, who can paint these puppets, are not easily available. Therefore, the old puppets have to be used for the old themes. This is the opinion of Kakappa of Kakanur.

There are no written texts for the leather-puppet performances. The themes are orally transmitted from generation to generation. These artists have a reverential attitude towards their art. Every New Moon Day and Full Moon Day, they offer *puja* to the leather-puppets. Similarly at the beginning of each play they offer prayers to Lord Ganesha and the village deity. After the prayer is over, the puppeteer explains the theme of the play briefly and prays to Lord Ganesha to ward off all the possible hindrances in the performance. (One may easily see the parallels between the leather-puppet shows and the *bayalatas*.) Then he thanks and praises all the people of the lane and their leaders, who have arranged the show with contributions from among themselves.

The literature of leather-puppet theatre is transmitted orally and hardly reduced to the written text. It consists of both prose and poetry. The puppeteer, who is a professional artist, knows his prose dialogues by heart. His eloquence is highly appreciable. His mastery over his voice, his ability to produce a variety of tones is remarkable. He cannot achieve originality in his prose dialogues every day. The songs sung by him are mostly composed by others and borrowed by him to suit the needs of the theme. But he goes on adding to the humour of the play by learning new jokes, proverbs and sentences after the gap of a few months.

The sentiments of heroism (*vira*), pathos (*karuna*) and humour (*hasya*) are commonly depicted by the leather-puppet theatre. Whenever the feelings of the characters reach high intensity, the prose dialogues culminate into beautiful songs sung to the accompaniment of musical instruments thereby capturing the hearts of the audience. The humorous element is depicted through ironical and satirical remarks and sometimes through absurd combination of thought and rhymes. Introducing humorous interludes right in the midst of the main theme is a characteristic feature of the leather-puppet performances. The humorous dialogues between the *killiketa* and his coquettish beloved, Bangarakka entertain the audience. Many times humour is tinctured with obscenity. The puppet, i.e. *killiketa*, attracts the attention of the audience with his peculiar shape, black complexion, snub-nose, thick lips, potbelly and crooked hands and legs.

Generally mythological themes from the *Ramayana*, the *Mahabharata*, the *Bhagavata* and other narratives are selected for leather-puppet performances. But nowadays even historical and social themes are depicted. The stories connected with mythical heroes and events like Vira Abhimanyu, Babhruvahana, Kichakavadha, Dashavatara, Parijata, Bhasmasura, Yayati, Rati-Kalyana, Girija-Kalyana, Sita-Swayanvara and Bhisma Vijaya are depicted by the Shadow Plays. There is frequent exchange of themes between Shadow Plays and *Baayalata* folk plays. Some adventurous troupes have presented Shadow Play performances on the lives of Basaveswara and Mahatma Gandhi.

Nowadays Shadow-Theatre is used by the Government of Karnataka for popularizing the Government politics and projects like literacy campaign, green revolution, health education, family planning and awareness about AIDS.

The language employed by the puppeteer is neither the standard one nor the folk one, but a golden mean between the two. It is occasionally peppered with descriptive patches and figures of speech. The puppeteer does not care for the purity of language or thought. On the contrary he can mix the profound with the profane, the ancient with the modern, the classical with the realistic, Sanskrit with English for the sole purpose of entertaining the audience. The abundant use of abusive words like whoreson, son of a bitch, curses and proverbs are common features of the language of Shadow Plays.

A distinct feature of the Shadow Plays of Hyderabad-Karnataka is the regional variety of language used in them. The major language employed in them is Kannada, but it is always mixed with either Telugu or Marathi or even Urdu in order to attract the audiences of the border areas of Karnataka, Maharashtra and Andhra Pradesh.

The chief value of a leather-puppeteer lies in his (mono-actor like) ability to utter a variety of dialogues of different characters by producing a variety of tones according to the situation. The audience think that the dialogues of different characters are spoken by different people, but the fact is that it is only the puppeteer sitting behind the curtain, who produces a variety of sounds and tones—like the heroic and the pathetic, the turbulent and the serene, the male and the female, the written and the colloquial, the old and the young.

While the puppeteer is speaking the dialogues from behind the curtain, the *tabla* (vertical drum) player sitting outside the curtain, will be responding to the former with his affirmative tags like 'yes, 'yes' and interrogative tags like 'What happened next?' and 'Is that so?'

Music is an inevitable part of puppet theatre. But there cannot be a simple answer to the question as to what kind of music is employed in this theatre. On the whole, three kinds of music are employed by different troupes. Some troupes employ purely folk music; some, semi-folk music and some others, classical music. In the early days, the members of back-chorus used to play *dholu* or *dholak*, but later *dholu* was replaced by the horizontal drum called *maddale* due to the influence of *bayalata* theatre. Similarly in the early days, they used to employ a drone-box called *'pavari,'* but later it was replaced by harmonium. But cymbals have continued to be employed in the present as in the past. A majority of puppeteers and members of back-choruses cannot afford to learn music systematically due to poverty.

There are many religious, cultural and social superstitions attached to the leather-puppet theatre of Karnataka. Some believe that they can get rains for their village by arranging a performance of the leather-puppet play. Some others believe that they can have the disease of their cattle cured by arranging a performance of such plays. Sometimes people get the leather-puppets of Rama, Sita or Krishna prepared and donate them to the director of puppet-theatre in memory of their elders or ancestors. The open praise of such donors by the director elicits further donations.

The leather-puppet theatre is found in every part of Karnataka except the coastal and rainy belt of the State. It is a domestic art and the puppets are multi-coloured. But the puppets of other States are only black and white.

The leather-puppets of northern Karnataka are not very big. They measure one and a half or two feet in height. The heroes represented by these puppets wear a cap, have a beard, hold a sword in hand and ride elephants or horses. There seems to have been the Muslim influence on the making of these puppets. The legs of these puppets are not flexible. The entire puppets are made to dance. The puppet player sits behind the curtain whereas the interpreter sits outside and interprets the story to the audience. Women join as back-chorus to the other male singers.

The puppets of southern Karnataka are slightly bigger than those of the north (yet of middling size). The main feature of these puppets is that the legs and hands of these puppets are flexible or movable. Therefore, the movements of such puppets are more dexterous and attractive than those of the immovable ones. Even the difficult actions like cutting the throat or other limbs (especially legs and hands) of the enemy can be shown through these puppets.

The leather-puppet theatre tradition of Andhra Pradesh and Karnataka border is very different from that of interior Karnataka, in that the puppets of the former are life-size in height and multi-coloured. This naturally requires a big stage and a good deal of ability on the part of the director, who cannot sit but has got to stand and control the puppets.

Dr. Shivram Karanth suspected that there might not be more than four or five troupes of *killiteta* performers. But recent facts discovered by the folk scholars show that there are a number of troupes in Karnataka which are not properly discovered, counted and recorded. According to present calculation, there are about 300 troupes of leather-puppet performers and about twenty-five troupes of string-puppet performers in Karnataka.

Some of the troupes of leather-puppet performers are said to be found in the villages like Akkihebbala, Tyapenahalli (near Nagamangala), Kadabahalli (near Bellur), Markonahalli, Ketuhalli (near Ramanagar), Mudugere, Bommalatapuram, Belagallu (Bellary district) and Binkadakatti and some villages of Belgaum, Dharwad, Hassan, Mandya, Mysore and Gadag districts.

We may have a glimpse of some well-known leaders of leather-puppet troupes in order to know the variety of methods and manner of performance. For example, Gomberama Hombayya has a repertoire of more than thirty-three *'prasangas'* (thematic units or events) connected with the *Ramayana* and the *Mahabharata*. His troupe takes a series of five nights for the performance of a few select events of the *Mahabharata* story.

His troupe has about five hundred leather-puppets equally divided by his four sons. All the members of the family except children know the dialogues of all the characters. They have got to get a curtain cloth of nine elbow-lengths only through begging. They decide the direction of the stage according to the astral time (*tithi*) and the theme of the play. Whenever the elderly man in the family cannot earn enough through such performances, his sons separate from him and start earning their own livelihood from their own independent performances. This is how the tradition has been kept up.

There is a family of *killiketas* in Gosabala village of Belgaum district, who have a land grant in recognition of their profession. They perform a leather-puppet play about the Pandavas on the day of Kartik.

Bharamappa and his family from Yadramanahalli gave a performance of an event of the *Ramayana* at the Kannada Department of Karnatak University, Dharwad, in October 1984. The performance began with praise of Lord Ganesha and Goddess Sharada followed by the meeting between Golla (milkman) and Gollati (milkmaid). This is the influence of the *sannata* (small-play) entitled *Sri Krishna Parijata.* There are also traces of the influence of the Jain *Ramayana*. Bharamappa's language is Marathi. He learnt the art from his maternal grandfather, maternal grandmother and uncle, Basappa of Morageri. He used the leather-puppets belonging to his ancestors. The *shanubhoga* of the village gave him a land grant in recognition of his art.

Bharamappa offers his own interpretation of the folk-myth of Jokumaraswami. According to him, Kyatappa is born earlier than Jokumara. His wife Bangarakka is naked. Kyatappa has a tuft of hair on his head and is a hero in the village. *Killiketa* is a director. Bharamappa has rights to perform his puppet-shows in thirty-three villages. He gets gifts from the villagers during the harvesting season. While receiving these gifts from the farmers, he utters the good wishes in a set poetic style.

According to Bharamappa, *killiketas* are of two kinds: domestic and fishermen. They worship the domestic deities like Huligemma, Yallamma, Kolashanta, Tipperudraswami, Kotturesha, Maddanaswami and Goni Basappa. They worship the leather-puppets on the festival days of Dasara and Ugadi. According to Bharamappa, the troupes of leather-puppets are available in villages like Odakalagi (Kudligi taluka), Garaga (near Maremmanahalli), Anakunti (Ranebennur taluka) and Hatti (Mulgund taluka). Once Bharamappa visited Russia for arranging performances by his troupe.

The parents and grandparents of Sayabanna Satabara of Gulbarga used to perform leather-puppet plays, though he has not learnt this art formally. But he has donated more than a hundred leather-puppets to Gulbarga University for preservation in the folk museum. Sayabanna's ancestors hailed from Devanagaon of Bijapur district.

Shankara is a *'kataba'* from Uduchana village of Afzalpur taluka of Gulbarga district. He performs the leather-puppet plays like his father and uncle. His relatives stay in Salotagi village of Bijapur district and have thousands of leather-puppets in their possession

Bhimappa of Bommanakheda village of Chincholi taluka, Bapu Kshetri and his son Rachu Kshetri and Maruti Uppar of Maindaragi village and Ramachandra of Karur village of Alanda taluka are well-known leather-puppet players. Rachu Kshetri and Maruti Uppar of Maindaragi village have written a *sannata* (small-play) entitled *Arabara Ata*. Both of them are good leather-puppet performers also. Whereas Rachu was an expert in singing, Maruti was an expert in playing *dappu* (small flat drum). They were also known for their creativity in adapting the *Arabara Ata* (*A Play about Arabs*) to the leather-puppet theatre and achieved great popularity by giving performances of this play in villages and towns like Madana-Hipparagi, Nimbaragi, Akkalakot and Maindaragi. Later the same theme was adapted to the *Gondaligya* narrative performances also. Both of them are disciples of a Muslim saint called Gaibi Pir.

Once upon a time Raichur district was known for leather-puppet theatre. Krishnappa of Kurdi village of Manvi taluka was an expert leather-puppet performer. He is known as Sillikyata Krishnappa. Even in his advanced age, he has been performing and teaching his art to a number of disciples. In 1986, he was honoured with an Award by the Janapada and Yakshagana Academy of the Government of Karnataka

Similarly Doddabalappa of Moranalli village of Koppala district and Doddabharamappa of Yadravi village of Hagaribommanahalli taluka of Bellary district were also honoured with Awards by the Janapada and Yakshagana Academy of the Government of Karnataka. It is a matter of pride for India that Doddabharamappa visited Germany and earned the appreciation of the German audience for his leather-puppet shows.

Belagallu Viranna is an important shadow-puppeteer, who has settled in Bellary and continued this art through his family tradition. He has been awarded the Karnataka Rajyotsava Prasasti, Karnataka Janapada Academy Prasasti and Janapadasri Prasasti in recognition of his excellent performances of leather puppets all over Karnataka and even beyond the State.

Gunduraj is another leather-puppeteer, who has settled in Huvinahalli Kavali in Hassan district. He has been engaged in the preparation of puppets, singing in the back-chorus and playing the puppets in collaboration with his father Gombe Ramayya right from his fifth year. He has been giving thousands of performances of other arts like playing on the harmonium, *Harikatha* and *Bhagavata* recitals. He has been honoured with the Karnataka Janapada Academy Award and many awards from many cultural associations. He has leather-puppets in his possession, which are about three hundred years old.

These artists, Belagallu Viranna and Gunduraj have been performing inside as well as outside Karnataka. The leather-puppets prepared by these artists have been exported to many foreign countries like Italy, England, America, Africa and Korea.

The Puppet Land of Bangalore and Ranga Putthali employ the puppets for the expression of dream element. Putthalika troupe of Kolkata has adapted *Ali Baba and Hundred Thieves* to leather-puppet theatre.

The leather-puppet theatre is neglected these days because of the onslaught of modern technological means of entertainment like film, television, radio, audio and video shows. The villagers, who have come under the influence of such modern media, do not show much interest in inviting the leather-puppet troupes to their villages. Some of the puppeteers have, therefore, been directing their art to propagandist programmes of the Government of Karnataka like family planning, pulse polio removal of AIDs and cancer, rural development, national pension scheme and literacy. On the whole, the leather-puppet theatre is on the verge of death. The precious art can be preserved only with the entry of educated people into the world of folk art, encouragement by organizations dedicated to folklore and the public patronage for the folk-artists.

It is a matter of satisfaction to note that the Government of Karnataka has been recognizing the talent of leather-puppet performers and encouraging them with prestigious awards. The five major Universities in Karnataka (at Dharwad, Gulbarga, Mysore, Mangalore and Bangalore) have been showing keen interest in the folklore studies. But the urgent need of the hour seems to be a willingness to introduce the practical training about the leather-puppet performance as a separate course in the postgraduate departments by appointing well-known artists in the field as it is done in the Universities of England, America,

Canada and other European countries. Similarly the Department of Kannada and Culture should create and maintain a database of all the artists (living and dead), their troupes and tools for the encouragement of further research in the field.

Bibliography

Biradar, M.G. *Janapada Samalokana,* Kalburgi: Chitkala, 1981.

Boralingaiah, H.C. *Karnataka Janapada Kalegala Kosha,* Hampi: Prasaranga, Kannada Visvavidyalaya, 1996.

Chidananda Murthy, M. *Gramina.* Bangalore: Bapco Prakasana, 1977.

Durgadas. K.R. *Ballary Jilleya Bayalatagalu*, Belagavi: Samata, 1996.

Gargi, Balwant. *The Folk-Theatre of India.* Washington: University of Washington Press, 1966.

Hiremath R.C. *Janapada Sahitya Darsana,* Part I. Dharwad: Karnatak University, 1974.

Imrapur, Somashekhara, *Janapada Vijnana.* Dharwad: Chetana, 1979.

Ittannavar, Srirama, *Sri Krisna Parijata: 0ndu Adhyayana.* Bilagi: Vini, 1991.

Kalburgi, M.M. *Marga*, 2 Vols. Bangalore: Naresh, 1988.

Kambar, Chandrasekhar, *Uttara Karnatakada, Janapada Rangabhumi.* Dharwad: Manvantara, 1965.

Krishnasharma, Betageri, *Kannada Janapada Sahitya*, Dharwad: Prasaranga, Karnatak University, 1976.

Latthe, M.S. *Bayalatada Sarathi.* Mutanal: Mallasarja Prakasana, 1978.

_____. *Janapada Kavicharite.* Dhangapur: Basavantarao Malipatil Memorial Publication, 1980.

_____. *Janapada Samsodhanatmaka Barahagulu.* Kalburgi: Patil Dal Mill, 1980.

Malasetty, Basavaraj, *Uttara Karnatakada Bayalatagalu.* Dharwad: Prasaranga, Karnatak University, 1983.

Marulasiddappa, K. *Adhunika Kannada Nataka*, Bengaluru: Ankita, 2002.

Mathur J.C. *Drama in Rural India.* New York: Asia, 1964.

Police-Patil, Basavaraj, *Hyderabad-Karnatakada Sannatagalu*, Gulbarga: Prasaranga, Gulbarga University, 1999.

Ranganath H.K. *The Karnataka Theatre*. Dharwad: Karnatak University, 1960.

Sunkapur, M.S. *Janapada Sahitya Darsana,* Part II and III. Dharwad: Prasaranga, Karnatak University, 1976.

Thurston, Edgar. *Castes and Tribes of Southern India*, Vol. III, Delhi: Cosmo, 1975.

Ulbricht, H. *Wayang Purwa*. Kuala Lumpur: Oxford University Press, Rpt. 1972, p. xv.

An Existential Approach to Folk Elements in Basavaraj Naikar's *Sangya-Balya*

BHAGABAT NAYAK
Kandarpur College, Siddheswarpur, Cuttack

Indian English drama had its beginning in the nineteenth century with the publication of Krishna Mohan Banerjee's *The Persecuted* (1931). But the real foundation for the Xanadu of Indian English drama was given by Sri Aurobindo, Rabindranath Tagore and T.P. Kailasam in the pre-Independence period. Apart from a number of dramatists in English, the plays of a host of dramatists in 'Bhasha' (G.N. Devy's term) literatures have been transcreated (P. Lal's expression) into English by the dramatists in their bilingual endeavour or translated by others in the post-Independence period. However, these plays from 'Bhasha' literatures form a substantial part of Indian English drama. Indian English drama as a whole deals with India's historical past, legends, folklores, myths, contemporary subject matters and social realism with universal appeal. It has flourished with eminent dramatists like Girish Karnad and Mahesh Dattani in recent times. The plays of Badal Sircar, Vijay Tendulkar and Pratap Sharma in Bhasha literatures have been translated into English for their pan-Indian realism. Their plays have drawn the attention of international audience. Yet many such plays are there in Bhasha literatures which need much care to be translated into English and they are really the undiscovered assets for Indian English literature.

Basavaraj Naikar, Professor of English at Dharwad University, a creative writer, critic, translator and educationist, has made an attempt to translate some Kannada literary texts into English for their pan-Indian reality and universal appeal, and with an intention to give them international publicity. As a translator he has remained true to the original texts and sometimes his translations become more powerful and forceful than the original texts. The oral text of *Sangya-Balya: Betrayal* was originally composed by Rayappa Pattar. It is a popular folk play of North Karnataka often staged in the form of *sannata* (small play) or *dappinata* (drum play). Naikar has taken the context of the play from the oral text recited by Basavanagouda Patil, Gangappa Mulimani and Fakirappa Madiwalar of Mutanala village in Belgaum district. Although its written form was published by Mallikarjuna Latthe of Gulbarga University in 1991, it is successfully translated into English by B.S. Naikar. During important fairs, festivals and cultural celebrations, the play is being staged in northern Karnataka districts and captures the attention of the educated and fashionable people of the cities as well as in rural areas. Naikar has been inspired by Balwant Gargi's dismissal of the folk theatre of North-Karnataka in his book *The Folk-Theatre of India* due to lack of proper information but it has developed his interest both as a translator and research oriented folklorist.

In this age of science and technology people may have lost their interest in studying folklores, legends and myths but Naikar has tried his best to focus on them in his native culture and tradition with social realism, and often with pan-Indian and cosmopolitan touch. Through translation he imagines to communicate his vision transcending all linguistic barriers. He writes in his 'Introduction' to the play: "I undertook the translation of this play into English as I feel that the elemental theme ingrained in it has universal appeal and therefore deserves international publicity. . . . The texture of the play, a mixture of prose and poetry, has been brought out in the present translation quite clearly, though alas, the melody and rhythm of the original

Kannada poetry cannot ever be dreamt of being expressed, even partially" (xii-xiii).

The play has all the folk elements of songs, tales, riddles, proverbs, myths, legends, superstitions and ballads which are prevalent in rural areas. In the portrayal of the incidents in life he has projected taboos, indecency, profanity and vulgarity for its aesthetic perfection. Folk literature is "the traditional literature of the unlettered mass living in one integrated social group. It is orally transmitted and can be claimed to be 'of the people, by the people, for the people" (Bhattacharyya 677). But "Folk-drama is another element in folk-literature which can be found in some form or other in the various states of India" (692). Folk-drama leads us to the unsophisticated world of our tradition, heritage and culture where the unlettered masses enjoy it. Folk drama has different names in different states but in totality there is the adoption of themes from the popular Indian epics and the puranas, and gradually folk-drama is becoming more secular in spirit while dealing with the traditional subjects. Although modern techniques are involved in it, contemporary social realism, political themes individuals' existential angst and modern stagecraft cannot be isolated from its traditional subjects. In Assam folk-drama is known as *ankiya*, in Andhra as *kuravanji*, in Bengal as *Yatra*, in Gujarat as *bhaoyani*, in Karnataka as *bayalata*, in Madhya Pradesh as *mach*, in Maharashtra as *tamasha* and in Orissa as *loknatya* but in its pan-Indian context folk-dramas deal with the subject matter and social realism in the portrayal of characters, incidents, conflicts, romance, laxity in conjugal bliss, economic relationship and wanderings in the labyrinths of woman's life.

This paper analyzes the folk elements in the play *Sangya-Balya* and focuses on the existential suffering of the characters. They take the responsibility as role models in their respective places and activities. They have their free choice of life, individual philosophy, personal ethics, loyalty, gratitude and belief in God. While analyzing them in the playwright's tragic vision, the paper focuses on their existential angst and sufferings. Existentialism is a twentieth century philosophical current that stresses personal responsibility and the relation of the individual to the universe or to God. The precursor of existentialist philosophy is the Danish philosopher, Soren Kierkegaard (1813-1855) who expressed this philosophical vision analyzing the plight of individual's condition which one cannot avoid or cannot avert in his real life. The later thinkers of this philosophy in the second half of twentieth century like Nietzsche, Heidegger, Sartre and Camus explain that existentialism defines human 'existence' that precedes his 'essence.' In general, existentialists emphasize on the fear and despair that the isolated individuals feel. Existentialism approaches the individual's existence and not his social or altruistic conditions. The existentialists hold the view that one's suffering begins with his sense of dread and despair that arise from his responsibility and decisions for his relationship with others. Most of the decisions, problems and questions in life are not accessible to reason because they are infinitely variable. Individuals assert or wilfully express their freedom to choose them in their human condition which finally affirms their destiny. Albert Camus rightly views in his *The Myth of Sisyphus* (1942): "It is indeed true that we are bound to our destinies, that there is no point struggling against them, even then this remains--that we do not submit passively . . . but with dignity and strength. Surely, this, to some extent, frees us from our bond" (246).

In everyday life the individual has to choose something good or bad for his life. Even the refusal to choose is a choice and this leads to his existential suffering because through this choice he expresses his mode of expression and freedom situating his 'self' between 'existence' and 'essence.' Existentialists argue that individuals have the liberty to accept the risk of responsibility and their commitment in their social and circumstantial situations, inexplicable absurdity and suffering. Jean-Paul Sartre writes: "We mean that man first of all exists, encounters himself, surges up in the world and defines himself afterward. If man, as the existentialist sees him, is not definable, it is because to begin with he is nothing. He will not be anything until later, and then he will be what he makes of himself" (Kaufmann 289).

Man is the maker of his own destiny. Destiny is bred out of his action and action follows choice and freedom. This is the reason why individual always has his choice for his action that builds his destiny which the individual cannot avoid or avert but to accept however it is favourable or relentless.

The central theme of *Sangya-Balya* is the role of elemental passion in interpersonal and human relationship. Ethical aspect in human relationship is embedded in the thematic concerns like illicit sex, crushing poverty and betrayal. The historicity of the theme of *Sangya-Balya* as a social play establishes controversy in its artistic presentation of vision about human relationship and values. In the portrayal of Ganga, the female protagonist and her existential suffering "some folk scholars of northern Karnataka are of the opinion that Pattar Master himself was in love with Ganga and when his love was not reciprocated by her, he took revenge on her by writing a play denigrating her character" (Naikar x). However, the anonymous playwright of Bailawadi village of Bailahongala taluka is still green in the folk memory for the heroine Gangi for whom Sangya was murdered and Irya was executed. For its social realism, colloquial flavour, lyrical delicacy, rhythmic sense and picturesqueness of imagery the play is widely popular in North Karnataka. Even Chandrasekhar Kambar's troupe has given a number of performances in Bangalore and K.V. Subbanna's opera-version has earned a great deal of popularity in Karnataka.

Realism in the play is expressed in the actual presentation of life. While demonstration of truth is the basic element in realism the dramatist as a realist sets out to write this play with common incidents and day-to-day affairs of life. He has presented life, habit, passion, love, strength, weakness, marriage, infidelity, betrayal, death, and search for happiness in the experiences of common and middle class people. The dramatist involves the subject matter that gives the readers the illusion of actual experiences. The theme is melodramatic and tragic not in Shakespearean sense but its extraordinariness is based on triviality, circumstantial and commonplace incidents. The dramatist renders the subject matter in casual manner that appeals common man's life. Existentialism may be unfamiliar but it reinforces an ethical awareness among the audience for the security of conscience. Hans Bertens writes: "Realism suggests that the characters that it presents find the reasons for their actions and decisions inside themselves" (7). Sangya (known as Sangappa and Sanganna) and Balya (known as Balanna and Balapa) are bosom friends. Sangya is the rich landlord of Bailahangala and Balya is his poor but loyal friend. Their friendship is exemplary in the locality. Although Sangya supports Balya financially on humanitarian grounds Balya expresses his loyalty to him on ethical grounds. The plot within the plot is woven intricately when friendship of Sangya and Balya has an effect on the matrimonial happiness of Virabhadra and his wife Ganga. Virabhadra (known as Virappa, Irappa or Irya), a dealer in pearls, gems and all kinds of precious stones goes away to Bellary on a business tour leaving his young wife Ganga in the care of Paramma, a mischievous lady of the village and two of his brothers Virupaksi and Basavanta. The rest becomes a tragedy. On the one hand the playwright has dealt with poverty, friendship, loyalty and values in human life, and on the other he deals with the theme of faithlessness, treachery, ungratefulness and betrayal. Apart from this belief in divinity, customs, traditions and religious rituals in individuals' faith the dramatist embellishes them in their existential awareness for a better integral and religious life.

Sangya, the protagonist is a rich landlord and shares his moments with his childhood friend Balya, who is financially dependent on him. But the flow of tempestuous passion for love with beauteous Ganga, the wife of the rich merchant Virabhadra, leads Sangya to his tragic end. The play is all set in the quaint village of Bailahongala. The circumstantial departure of Virabhadra to Bellary leaving his young wife Ganga at home becomes the turning point in his life. Ganga has been recurrently jilted and disturbed by Sangya and his paid pets. While all his attempts fail to convince Ganga to share her bed with him Sangya feels insulted and humiliated. His consultation with a *Karavanji* (a fortune-teller) and her advice to engage Paramma, the elderly lady whom Virabhadra had engaged to take care of Ganga, has been cunningly used to trap Ganga for Sangya. The five acts of the play appear to be five episodes and they form an organic whole to focus on individual's existential suffering with social realism.

The play begins traditionally with an invocation to Lord Ganapati, the son of Goddess Parvati and God Sambhu. Sutradhara, the professional master in stagecraft and stage activities, introduces the intimate and inseparable friendship of Sangya and Balya. The friendship of the two is known all over the city of Gadag and in the market places of Hongala. Both the friends are the lovers of Lord Basavanna of the Shapur Lane and they love to study Vedas, Shastras and Puranas. Sangya is rich with abundant gold and silver, milch cows and buffaloes but Balya is a wage-earner who goes to work to provide jowar to his children. In spite of this difference, their love for each other is so intense that one cannot bear other's absence for a moment. About Balya's absence, Sangya says: "I felt so bored without you. I did not relish my food or water . . . come on, let us chat with cheer" (18). Realizing Balya's misery in poverty Sangya takes him to the shop of a Marwari Sethji for some dhotis, shirt pieces and turbans. As the Marwari needs hard cash for payment,

Sangya leaves Balya there to bring some money. But due to his late arrival the Sethji applies his 'Marwari method' of treatment to Balya who is released later by Sangya in a precarious condition. The way of dealing in the masrai (thick cotton) and mulmul (thin cotton) items by the Sethji, his charging of "commission, shop rent, income tax and sales tax" (21) and Shylockian attitude towards the customers, Sangy's assistance to Balya, their plan to go to police, and Marwari's offering of clothes free of cost to them out of his fear for the police seem to be the real incidents. The incidents are visibly common but they are projected in a convincing manner.

The friendship between Sangya and Balya has a parallel development with the conjugal relationship between Virabhadra, the landlord, and his wife Ganga. Dealing with the extramarital relationship, promiscuity, hatred and betrayal, the dramatist unites the Sangya-Balya episode with the Virabhadra-Ganga episode that gives a steady growth to the plot. As the eldest brother Virabhadra has much concern for his two younger brothers—Virupaksi and Basavanta. He concentrates his mind on his business, agriculture and household. Receiving an invitation from the merchant Ramarao Sethji he immediately gets ready to Bellary on a business mission. Like every young man he is tempted by his wife's beauty and is prompted by the prospect of his business. He arranges Paramma, an elderly lady of his neighbourhood to give company to Ganga during his absence and orders his two brothers--Virupaksi and Basavanta--to look after family affairs and remain obedient to Ganga. He advises Virupaksi to take care of agriculture, and Basavanta, the wrestler, to guard the family. He promises to bring an excellent turban with golden treads for Virupaksi and beautiful silk knickers for Basavanta. Virabhadra is the perfect example of a *grahastha* who seems to be initiated in the theory of *karma*. He is a man of action and believes that "even a pot full of gold will not be enough for the livelihood of an idler" (30). His household managerial capacity, ambition in business, love for his wife and two brothers are exemplary. He knows Paramma, a mischievous woman but applies the reason that a known enemy is better than an unknown friend. This is the reason why he engages Paramma for Ganga's company during his absence. He wants her to keep Ganga engaged in eating, chatting, and sleeping till his return.

Virabhadra's family deity as well as the presiding deity of the locality is Basavanna. Virabhadra has all respect for the deity known for his fame in the entire world. At the time of his departure he advises Ganga to offer puja to Lord Basaveswara during the annual fair on the hillock. He reminds her that it is their family tradition to visit the annual fair of Lord Basavanna to get his blessings. Virabhadra, the man of strong will, belief and action has every reason to arrange Paramma for his household. Although her husband suspects her for her 'double talk' and 'coquettish' nature, Virabhadra takes her into confidence because of her old age. Like many old women, Paramma has her follies and foibles but she has her obligation to her family and social values. She goes to take her husband's permission to stay with Ganga who in his old age says to her: "I can spend the day and night easily/ If you are within the fold of my arms" (34). In her reaction Paramma views her plight with her husband, "I have to live with such a queer husband" (33). This reveals Paramma's suffering. She thinks that her husband has no doubt over her character but he must have asked Paramma to guard the wealth of the family.

Existentialism is a recent trend. The artist projects it in the analysis of the events, situations and actions in the life of the characters consciously or unconsciously. At the same time through the psychoanalysis of the characters the dramatist focuses this in their suffering. After Virabhadra's departure Ganga and Paramma remain busy for some time at home in the preparation of *holige* (sweet pickle) and then prepare the items like water, oil, vibhuti, bel leaves, camphor, fruits, consecrated food, incense and wick lamp to offer as oblations for God's boon through puja. They visit the temple of Lord Basaveswara covering a long distance. They get surprised to see the temple where people sing in chorus the glory of Lord Siva. Basaveswara is famous for his vibhuti and rudraksi for which devotees make a rush. The glory of the fair is marked with the glamour of Ganga. Her physical glamour disturbs the psyche of the devotees and they talk about her lemon-complexion, lotus eyes, elephant-gaited walk and bewitching beauty. Even she has become the object of attraction for the lascivious priests in the temple. While Sangya and Balya are watching the temple car of God Basaveswara being pulled by the devotees they discover Ganga, 'a veritable goddess Rati,' 'like a royal parrot' was swinging her arms in style.

Role of fate has its arbitrariness in the existential condition of the individual characters. Fate has its role in Ganga's missing of his necklace in the fair and its accidental finding by Sangya gives a turning point to the plot. As Shakespeare dropped a handkerchief in *Othello* and helped Desdemona and the Black Moor to suffer, similarly Ganga lost her necklace and it led to the tragic catharsis for Sangya and Virabhadra. The dramatist uses this incident symbolically for Ganga's losing of heart to a man other than her husband. Sangya's returning the necklace to Ganga and showing favour to her in an obliging way are certainly love for him in her heart. As his passion's slave, Sangya becomes 'thought sick' and eccentric that leads him to 'bestial oblivion.' With a filthy mind, he imagines: "Her arms were like creepers and her thighs, like plantain trunks; her eyes were like lotus petals and her cheeks, like a mirror; her breasts were like lemons and her teeth, like pomegranate seeds" (49). Sangya comes to know through Balya that she is Ganga whose parents belong to Bailawada and her husband Virabhadra of Lagali family belongs to Bailahongala. A religious place is sacred for one to remove his maya (illusion) but in case of

Sangya it creates an illusion for Ganga. He almost faints on seeing her beauty and prays to Lord Sankara for the love of Ganga. He feels as if without Ganga and without her company his life is meaningless. He plans to gain Ganga's favour by any means. Being a married person having children also, he knows that it is unethical on his part to eye another's wife but his elemental passions make him suffer.

Balya plays the role of a pet while working under Sangya. As his friend and philosopher, he reminds Sangya about its consequence:

> Dear friend Sanganna,
> Ravana lost his heart to another's wife
> And consequently lost everything.
> Lest you should suffer like him,
> Remove the idea from your mind and
> Forgive me for giving you a piece of my mind. (49)

Sangya who stands for his values and generosity suspends his virtues wilfully for Ganga and engages Balya to earn Ganga's favour for him. Although at first Balya refuses to be a go-between finally he accepts it for his friend's sake. But Balya is more philosophic than his obsessive friend Sangya. He does not feel it wise to visit Ganga's house for his friend without any rhyme or reason. He is convinced that Ganga is a chaste woman; persuading her for another man is a dangerous task. Sangya has a cynical approach to womanhood. To him 'beauty,' the strength of a woman, is a weakness. He believes that beauty is a woman's virtue but it makes her weak and flexible. One is reminded here of John Donne's lines:

> Ride ten thousand days and nights,
> Till age show white hairs on thee,
> Thou, when though return'st, wilt tell me
> All strange wonders that befell thee,
> And swear
> Nowhere

Lives a woman true, and fair. (*Song* L.12-18)

and Shakespeare's phrase "Frailty, thy name is woman." Balya's visit to Ganga with Sangya's proposal was a failure. He is offended, harassed and punished for his misdemeanour but he becomes apparently happy at Ganga's 'sterling moral character' and her refusal of Sangya's proposal.

Balya's failure to brainwash Ganga disappoints Sangya. While visiting her, he asks her not to bother about the business of life. He explains her philosophy of life, its mundaneness and realizes her life as a physical being first and moral being second: "I, therefore, beg for your love. Please, give me the pleasure of union. After all, this mortal life is a temporary one, which is short-lived like a market day" (63). In response to his words and unusual suffering, Ganga warns him as a chaste wife: "Don't you remember the story of Kama? How Kama lusted after the woman and was burnt to ashes by Lord Shiva" (63). Ganga reminds him of his duty towards his wife and children and advises him to mend his behaviour without involving in nasty thoughts. Ganga appears as a 'stringed puppet' for Sangya without any iota of deficiency for her 'wonderful complexion.' Ganga tells him, "I am a chaste wife of my husband. If you ever touch me, you will suffer like a monkey feeding on lime paste" (64). Ganga appears like a "Royal belle with gentle gait" (65). Sex is spiritual but sexuality is a perversion. Sangya's sexual desire for Ganga makes him a perverted being. He has gone mad for her and any attempt by Sangya to seduce her would earn the result that Ravana had after abducting Sita and Dushasana had for disrobing Draupadi. Sangya, like a firefly, enters into the lamp to become a nincompoop.

Sangya takes the help of a *Koravanji* (the fortune-teller) to win the favour of Ganga. The *Koravanji* becomes an interpreter of maladies who promises him to cure the ills of his life by telling about the future of his love for Ganga:

I know how to bring together
Men and women and also
How to separate them cleverly.
I know how to mesmerize women
And make them follow you, men. (68)

With *Koravanji's* advice Sangya engages Paramma to seduce Ganga and in exchange of this he promises her to give a pair of buffaloes, a pair of saris, a pair of blouses and promises her to look after her family. Paramma is Machiavellian, jealous and intolerant of Ganga's beauty and happiness. She stands wholly outside the world of morality. Paramma tells Ganga that Sangya is handsome, generous and the villagers of Hongala marvel at his success. Paramma is coquettish by nature and knows how to tempt and trap other women. She tries her best to minimize Ganga's concern for her chastity and influences her not to be so conscientious. She supports her argument with the statement: "The rich man always maintains a mistress in addition to a wife" (74). Ganga's respect for Paramma disappears and she calls her a 'foolish bitch' for her ill-teaching.

Balya and Paramma play an important role in the development of the plot. Both the pets become destiny makers for Sangya and Ganga. They express their human depravity in their betrayal. Paramma feels insulted for her inability to tempt Ganga. At last she hits upon a plan of bringing Ganga round by blackmailing her. Accordingly, she brings in Sangya's turban and keeps it on Ganga's bed without her knowledge. Showing it to her, she threatens that she would disclose and publicize the matter to the whole village. Just playing her trick she says to Ganga: "I am not aware of how you have been carrying on with Sangya secretly. Shall I tell Virupaksi and Basavanta all about your secret love affair? Let Virabhadra come, I shall make him shave your head . . . And yet you pretend ignorance about it? . . . Your trick is like that of a grand-daughter teaching her grandmother how to cough" (74).

Ganga is flabbergasted and is mortally afraid of the possible scandal. For her Sangya is an 'existing subject' and Virabhadra is a 'thinking subject.' She, therefore agrees to oblige Paramma and asks her in riddles to bring along Sangya to her house at night "when the stone slab is vacant" means "when all those sitting on the stone slab outside their homes should have gone inside," "when wood is joined to wood" means "when the doors of houses are shut"; and "when the jasmines begin to bloom" means "when the stars begin to twinkle in the sky" (75). Ganga falls a victim to her existing situation. Paramma succeeds in her cunning method to weaken Ganga and advises her: "You are a young lady. You know how to make the best of your youth." (75)

The illicit love affair between Ganga and Sangya continues for some time. By and by Sangya realizes his misdeed and evil habit of seducing another man's wife. He confesses before Ganga, 'I somehow feel disgusted with the whole thing, now" (76) but nothing is left for him to rethink. Ganga invites Sangya, "come on, let us go and mount the bed and satisfy our deep desire" (78) in a sweet siesta falling into each other's arms beneath a pair of shawls. Sangya welcomes her invitation in a romantic mood and says, "my beloved Ganga, I had waited for this meeting for such a long time, I simply cannot make out if it is a dream or reality" (77). The love affair between Ganga and Sangya becomes a matter of gossip in the village. The village folk whisper, prophesying the future of Sangya, the deceiver. The impending tragedy appears to be a world of action, and action is the translation of thought into reality.

The violation of chastity is the cause of tragedy in the play. Sangya's attraction for another man's wife is improper, Ganga's yielding to sexual temptation and susceptibility to sexual emotions, and Balya's treachery towards Sangya are several instances of the fallibility of human life. Virabhadra has a dream about his wife's misdeed. He returns to Ganga before time but what he heard from the villagers comes true when he discovers the criminal inside his house along with his wife. Although Sangya managed to escape in the darkness his turban in the room proved her betrayal to her husband. Virabhadra did not listen to Ganga's pleadings. He became wild for Ganga's destroying the sanctity of their matrimony and wanted to take revenge on Sangya for his wounded reputation. Suspecting that something has gone wrong, Balya laments in 'fear and pity' over the future of his friend Sangya: "In the beginning itself I warned Sangya against it, but he did not listen to me. I am also a poor fellow. I, therefore, joined hands with him. I think I may also suffer the consequences of this, as a Sanyasi has to suffer the consequence of a prostitute's sin. I am sure Sangya will have to face the blade of sickle. Let him face the music. However, can I oppose him? He is, after all, my friend who feeds me and gives me sufficient money for my livelihood. I am suffering from this self-created fear and wander about here and there in the village. Wherever I go, I hear people gossiping about Ganga and Sangya and their love affair" (79).

The tragic flaw leads to nemesis. Both Ganga and Balya become apprehensive of the future of Sangya. Irya is convinced of his wife's adultery and betrayal. Coming back to his sense he thinks that killing a woman is a heinous sin. He, therefore, orders his two brothers to confiscate Ganga's clothes and ornaments and send her to her father's house. He is determined to take revenge on Sangya who has cuckolded him. He sends his brothers to fetch Balya. Virabhadra loses self-control in his ravenous thirst for revenge. He promises Balya enough money, sixteen oxen, a sturdy cart and landed property to conspire with Sangya. Although he did not agree to betray his friend who has fed him all along his life with food and milk, he agrees to do it with Irya's warning in a survival strategy.

Balya's situation compels him to betray his friend Sangya. In fear and greediness he promises Virabhadra to bring Sangya accordingly on the way to Bailawada, the village of Ganga, during the Naga Panchami festival. Balya betrays Sangya on two levels: first he destroys Ganga's letter to Sangya sent by a messenger and prepares another in the name of Ganga with her invitation to go to Bailawada for Naga Panchami occasion; and secondly, he helps the three brothers--Virabhadra, Virupaksi and Basavanta--to ambush Sangya behind the *kevada* thicket who wait to kill him with axes and sickles. Ganga had come to know about Balya's betrayal to Sangya but it was Sangya's misfortune that he could not get her letter as Balya had received it from the messenger identifying himself as Sangya. When Sangya and Balya are on the way to Bailahongala, Balya, according to the plan, asks Sangya to wait for a while until he relieves himself. Now with his signal, the three brothers encircle Sangya and murder him. The brothers go to the police station and confess their guilt before the authority. Character is destiny. The doer only gets what he deserves.

The tragic end of Sangya is affected by the inexorability of the moral law of life. Sangya violates the moral principles and destroys the sanctity of matrimony. Ganga is punished for her adultery and betrayal of her husband. She is destined to live in forced celibacy in her parents' house. Her status of a 'respectable wife' is turned to a 'shameless whore.' The two sides of her character are expressed when she pretends to prove her innocence and purity of love for Virabhadra:

> Don't charge me unnecessarily
> And enjoy the fun my dear husband,
> I do not know anything
> That you charge me with.
> Don't do me any injustice
> By having baseless doubts. (84)

At the same time for her adultery, perjury, pretension and betrayal, Virabhadra calls her a "whore" appropriately when she says to Sangya realizing the impending danger:

> Don't you get worried, my Sangya,
> Listen to my promise. . . .
> I have fallen deeply in love with you,
> Our union has been sweet like milk and ghee
> Fie on my bad luck, I don't like my husband
> I shall sunder my relation with him
> Tomorrow itself. I don't care for what
> The people of the village might say. (82)

In the aftermath of the play Virabhadra is hanged to death by the British government in India on the charge of murder. His two brothers Virupaksi and Basavanta are exonerated on the condition that they be converted to Christianity.

As a folk drama *Sangya-Balya* focuses on the sufferings of the characters. The play conveys a message that betrayal is the cardinal sin for which its perpetrators meet their tragic end. The dramatist focuses on individuals' quest for 'moral autonomy.' The play conveys a moral in its tragic vision for a good number of Sangyas, Gangas, Virabhadras, Balyas and Parammas who in their everyday life fall victim to passion, temptation, revenge, greed, betrayal, cynicism and insanity of vindictiveness.

Works Cited

Bertens, Hans. *Literary Theory: The Basic*. NY: Routledge, 2001

Bhattacharyya, Ashutosh. "Folk Literature of India," *The Cultural Heritage of India*, Vol. V, ed. Suniti Kumar Chatterji. Calcutta: The Ramakrishna Mission Institute of Culture, 1978.

Camus, Albert. *The Myth of Sisyphus*. Harmondsworth: Penguin, 1984.

Naikar, Basavaraj S. *The Folk Theatre of North Karnataka*. Dharwad: Karnataka University, 1996.

_____. *Sangya-Balya: Betrayal*. New Delhi: Minerva Press, 2004.

Sartre, Jean-Paul. "Existentialism is Humanism," *Existentialism from Dostoevsky to Sartre*, ed. Walter Kaufmann. Cleveland: Blackwell, 1956.

The Lost Cultural and Traditional Identity of Indian Lore in Third World Literature: A Study of Sujatha Vijayaraghavan's *Hundred Tamil Folk and Tribal Tales*

RAGHAVI PRIYA J.
Res. Sch., School of Social Sc. and Langs., VIT, Vellore
LAXMI DHAR DWIVEDI
Asso. Prof., School of Social Sc. and Langs., VIT, Vellore

There are various types of cultural and traditional practices in India and other places which are interwoven into our society and religion. If we take India alone, it is in a humongous level; and thus hard to keep a written record of each and every cultural and traditional practice because most of them are found only in oral format. The only way through which our heritage, along with its culture and traditions, could be carried forth to the generations to come, was through 'Folktales' or 'Folklore' or folk literature, oral tradition, and through 'Tribal Tales' which were the best way of spreading knowledge to the illiterate and tribal clans. It is transmitted by word of mouth and consists of narrations in prose as well as verse; it also has poems, songs, myths, dramas, rituals, proverbs and riddles.

The recurrent theoretical question asked by many theorists and critics is, "Is folklore and tribal lore beyond preservation for future generations?" Many youths of our generation are unaware of the traditional value of 'Folklore.' They are not accustomed to it due to globalization and are living in a fast-paced world based on e-commerce and e-technology. Oral literature and oral form of telling tales is a tradition which is disappearing in the 21st century.

These issues can be seen using the postcolonial theory and gender discourse. For example, in old Tamil literature, the epic *Ramayana* has a lot of sub-plots based on the folklore of that century. It shows how rich our political and social system was then. It also has stories like how the squirrel got its three stripes, the test of fire which developed into the tradition of Sati; and why one should not cage a parrot. But there are many forms of telling "Ramayana." It started with the rich tradition of "Oral Tales"; even before it was written by Kambar, it had many different narrations of the same story. As each place has added its own traditional and local culture and flavour to the original story, we have as many as "1000 Ramayanas."

Colonialism has eroded the cultural and traditional sheen of India and with it the rich tradition of lore in the so-called context of the third world nations.[1] So, what is Folklore in the modern-day world? As Merriam says: "Folklore is the body of expressive culture, including tales, music, dance, legends, oral history, proverbs, jokes, popular beliefs, customs, and so forth within a particular population comprising the traditions (including oral traditions) of that culture, subculture, or group. Traditional customs, beliefs, stories, and sayings: ideas or stories that are not true but that many people have heard or read."

Sujatha Vijayaraghavan is a professor of English in Pondicherry University and has written Tamil fiction and poetry as well as translated many into English. *Hundred Tamil Folk and Tribal Tales* is one of her translation works. In this, we see a beaming cause to save folklore and tribal tales for future generations. It is a translation of "Naatupura Kathai Kalanjiyam" compiled and edited by Aaru Ramanathan. It is a collection of popular folk and tribal tales from all over Tamilnadu. Vijayaraghavan has separated the tales according to the districts they were gathered from and the region of their origin. The tales revolve around themes like "Tribal lore--independent literature," "The carnivalesque," "ancient cities and tales," and "folk dances."

The Folklores and Tribal tales have been an integral part of our culture and heritage since ages. When it comes to Indian folktales, it is found intertwined in this land filled with diverse religions, languages, cultures, castes and creeds and a land where tales and short stories are found in an everlasting range. Indian folklore and tribal tales have a wide range of stories filled with mythological legends, which surfaces from all walks of life. The interesting stories range from the remarkable *Panchatantra*, *Hitopadesha*, *Vikram and Vetal* to *Jataka* and *Akbar and Birbal*; it also follows the great Indian epics the *Ramayana* and the *Mahabharata*. Religious scripts like *Bhagavad Gita*, *Vedas* and *Upanishads* are full of didactic stories inspired by the lives of great men and saints. Indian folklore has perfect moral stories for children. All these ancient stories have been passed from generation to generation, from the old to the young through oral form, creating bonds of traditional values with their present-day generation.

> Surely no other discipline is more concerned with linking us to the cultural heritage from the past than is folklore; no other discipline is more concerned with revealing the inter-relationships of different cultural expressions than is folklore; and no other discipline is so concerned . . . with discovering what it is to be human. It is this attempt to discover the basis of our common humanity, the imperatives of our human existence that puts folklore study at the very centre of humanistic study. (Wilson 101)

Folklore is an unrecorded, unofficial, tradition of oral communication by word of mouth from one person to another; it gives importance to both the form and content of our traditions. It embraces all knowledge, moral and ethical values, attitudes, assumptions, feelings and beliefs transmitted by examples of either real or imaginary stories or a mix of both telling the stories of human and animals. But this richness is lacking in our present-day generation which is concerned with social media such as Facebook, WhatsApp, Twitter, Viber and so on; which in reality are not social in context. The physical connection and contact are lost between a child and a mother, a grandmother and a grandchild; as gone are the days of 'Nila Sooru,'[2] when the mother used to feed the child showing the moon and telling stories about gods, goddesses, poochaandis.[3] Nowadays grandchildren don't go to their grandma to hear stories of mythical characters or 'Thalattu song.'[4] Many times our rich literary culture is lost in transition because of the so-called 'third world' tag which we have been carrying all these years. But due to some pioneer folklorists in contemporary India like the father of "Indian Folklore" A.K. Ramanujan and other Indian folklorists like Jawaharlal Handoo, Sadhana Naithani, Anjali Padhi, Nandini Sahu, Mariamma Chedathy, Gambhari Devi, Verrier Elwin, Komal Kothari, K.K.N. Kurup, P.R. Thippeswamy, Ki. Rajanarayanan, Dinesh Chandra Sinha, Komal Swaminathan; and editors like Aaru Ramanathan, Dr. G. Stephen, T. Nadarajan and translators like A.K. Ramanujan and Sujatha Vijayaraghavan (Wiki), we have got back a part of our lost vibrant folklore and tribal tales.

In Sujatha Vijayaraghavan's *Hundred Tamil Folk and Tribal Tales*, we see the first set of tales from the regions around Cuddalore and the theme is "Gender and Divinity." It includes the popular "Anandayi" tales; the translator points out how Anandayi is worshipped only by women and is a woman turned into a goddess by the local women. In "The Foolish King" we see an Irulatchi becoming a queen and how human beings had direct contact with gods and goddesses. In stories like "Who can be Trusted," "The Creator's Knot" we see the tradition of village elders as the justice provider to the victims, just like our Panchayat system.

The story "Speak after You Look Before and Behind You" is a perfect example of how bribery can change even the gods. It is a story about how Lord Pillayar sides with the monkey which had shattered a sparrow's nest because the sparrow told the monkey that it was suffering in the rain due to its laziness. Pillayar supports the monkey because he received the bribe of one ripe jackfruit: "Well! Money reaches even the Netherworlds, if need be" (23). It is a moral folktale.

There are tales that deal specifically with Tamil beliefs and literature. The "Kuttiandavar" tale gives details of the glorious port city of Caveripoopatinam, it also shows the origin of the word city and urban people, as in those days it seems that the name "pattinam" or city only referred to Caveripoopatinam and the people was referred to as "pattanathar." Vijayaraghavan draws our attention to the fact of "the little canon shaping the big" and explaining how scholars hold the view that the literary classic, *Silappadikaran* "grew from folklore." In this story, she shows how the cast Chettiyar came about and how some rivers and ponds in Poompuhar could cure diseases like leprosy, tuberculosis and one such pond called Agni Kundam at Osarappar temple is capable of curing any level of poison if you just take a dip in it. Till today no one has died of poison or snake bite in Poompuhar. Thus, it proves that there is some kind of truth in folktales. It also gives us a rich description of our seaports and trade.

The series, "The Female Goddess: Consent and Dissent Narratives," shows how women were too chaste as the character Duruvathayi seen in "The God who Tested His Wife," who lives with her husband who is a chauvinist god in disguise of a man with leprosy as he wants to test his wife of her chastity. The story "When are you Going to Die," shows a witty mother-in-law who wins over her daughter-in-law without fighting with her. The story "Serving Food in a Clay Bowl" shows how one day we are going to get old and what we sowed will be returned to us by the future generation. "His mother became an old woman in due course of time. The boy who was now a married man called his wife and instructed to bring the clay bowl from the banana patch and serve the old woman food in it. The wife did as she was told." (54)

"The Smart One" and "The Pleasure with Madhavi" show the tradition of riddling and placing bets to check who the intelligent one is. "Footprints" and "Beating with the Broom" show how wrong decision skills can lead one into troubled waters.

"About Giving Alms" shows us the tradition of giving alms to the Brahmins, which is sometimes misused by that clan. It also shows how one must be generous only to the needy and poor. "A Knock with the Pestle" also deals with a similar issue but it is a story which talks about the traditional value of giving food to the poor as according to lore it may even save us our life and secure a place for us in heaven.

The Tamil specifics are also brought in with reference to folk deities such as Ayyanar and Jakkamma, sports such as Jallikattu, and dances such as Kummi. It has 100 tales which deal with mythology, moral values, wit, parables, religions, customs, beliefs, knowledge, riddles and songs with values. It shows both the bright and gloomy sides of our tradition and customs. It shows how both men and women can be selfish and cruel, as well as loving, caring and helpful.

There is a distinct identity of our traditions and cultures as well as universality about folktales. The folktale "The Foolish King" is about a sister who saves her brothers and this tale has striking similarities to that of Hans Christian Andersen's fairytale, "The Wild Swans" where the girl silently makes shirts for her brothers who have been turned into birds by their wicked stepmother. The story of the jealous neighbour who tries to imitate the journey to the forest and gets thrashed by bandits is another that has universal tone. In "The Tale of Tales," there is even a reference to "Chakespiyar" (Shakespeare). The chants and songs have been translated retaining the local flavour. Any attempt to document the richness of indigenous culture is appreciable in a globalised world, which is felt to be losing many of its distinct ethnic and cultural forms, languages, and performing styles. Sujatha Vijayaraghavan has spread this book to a wider audience through her translation.

If we ask ourselves the recurrent question asked by many, "Is folklore and tribal lore beyond preservation for future generations?," our answer would be a big "NO," because our folklore history is filled with world-renowned tales compilation like *The Hitopadesha* composed by Narayana Pandit around a thousand years ago, *The Jataka Tales* originally written in Pali language by Buddhist monks in 300 B.C, *The Panchatantra* a legendary collection of short stories from India originally composed in the 2nd century B.C by Vishnu Sharma along with many other scholars. After all these centuries still, they are looked upon as something valuable and resourceful by some of the readers and even writers like A.K. Ramanujan, Sujatha Vijayaraghavan, Komal Swaminathan and others. They are the "treasurers" of our "culture, traditions and heritage" of our nation. Their works should be preserved and protected and not discarded as simple third world writing. The folklore and tribal tales have universal concepts which are useful to all. It is a known fact that the people of the so-called Third World share a common historical background of colonialism and this experience makes the themes that the folktales address in a convincing way.

The translator in her preface points out how 'Eurocentric' emphasis is on the text of the other or the third world nations, especially their disregard of folktales as a cheap inferior thing and how "Contemporary folklore studies questions this attitude not only pointing to the colonial/ imperial impact upon research but also upon us, the country, at large where the same attitude kept and keeps the divide alive." (xxiii).

To conclude, the lost cultural and traditional identity of Indian lore as seen in third world literature is reviving slowly but steadily. We must be ready to shed our "cannibalism" and get in touch with our roots, our traditions. We must take pride in showcasing our folklore and tribal tales like the rest of the third world nations. Folktales are the only means through which society and social contact can be formed.

NOTES

1. The non-aligned nations like Africa, Asia, and Latin America which are often developing nations. They are in a "third" group of nations because they were allied neither with the United States nor with the former Soviet Union.
2. The food fed to the child under the full moon or just under the night sky, while telling various folk or tribal tales, to amuse the child.
3. Poochaandi are just the Tamil version of Bogeyman. In Tamilnadu, poochaandi is a word that is used to scare children, to make sure they sleep early, or to get them to eat properly. You will often hear mothers saying, "Poochaandi varan. He will take you away." He is given descriptions of someone looking ferocious and scary and who will come and take away misbehaving children.
4. It means lullaby sung to a baby.

Bibliography

Sujatha Vijayaraghavan, trans. *Hundred Tamil Folk and Tribal Tales*. New Delhi: Orient Blackswan, 2010.

Wilson, William A. "The Deeper Necessity: Folklore and the Humanities," *Journal of American Folklore* (1988): 101.

Chandrasekhar Kambar's *Sirisampige*: A Folk Play with Mythological Content

NASREEN BANU JAMADAR
G.F.G. College, Naregal

In folk literature the importance of the storyteller is stories, in oral traditions created thousands of years ago, no one knows the first storytellers; new storytellers add and change details, cultural perspective and viewpoints are shaped by storyteller's background and experiences. The central idea, message, or insight about life that the stories convey are universal themes; themes that are repeated across many cultures and over many time periods which express insights into life that many people understand. For example: the struggle of good against evil, moral—a lesson about life that is stated directly, usually at end of story. The folk form of literature is used to teach or to entertain.

Sirisampige is a folk play by Chandrasekhar Kambar who is a leading poet, playwright, folklorist, film director in Kannada language and the founder Vice-Chancellor of Kannada University in Hampi. He was born on January 2, 1937 at Ghodageri village in Belagavi district, Karnataka. Right from his young age, he evinced keen interest in folk arts, local culture and rituals. He felt comfortable with north Karnataka dialect of Kannada and relied on it for his poems and plays. His skilful use of the dialect in his plays and poems placed him on par with the stalwarts of the day.

Kambar cherishes the experiences of ordinary people and their unique rituals. "Chandrasekhar Kambar, steeped in the folk traditions of the region, has been most innovative in form, using songs, recitation, movement and rituals" (Hochman 1984) and he has written "more than twenty plays in Kannada, some socio-political, such as *Jokumaraswami* and *Rishyashringa*, and more recently comedy, such as *Sirisampige* (Dinkgrafe and Dinkgrafe 2002).

Kambar defies logic in most of his plays and tries to reflect the intricacies of the world through them. As he finds the complex network of life that evades concrete meaning, he faithfully reflects the same in his plays. A reader must not try to read his plays with the curiosity of a scientist to discover facts through logical reasoning. "An apparently wild opulence is what greets the reader as he delves into Kambar's writings. It is better that the reader relaxes into that opulence. For if he insists on taking a framework of logic into his reading, then that very frame might trip him up" (Taranath 1989). The lack of logic does not deter a reader or a spectator from sharing the message of the author. On the other hand, it helps the author capture the neglected aspect of human life.

Kambar borrows the texture of his plays from the environment and faithfully reflects it through his plays. In 'My Writing,' Kambar proclaims that "I draw my texture of experience mainly from my *sense of place*. It forms the main core of my writing. It gives me every ingredient of texture . . . . Environment, to me, comes primarily as a sense of place." He belongs to the class that observes and learns from its environment. The people of the class try to preserve their own tradition through art forms such as oral and written.

In a sense, not belonging to the upper class has helped him enormously. His people, illiterate and oppressed, sang to preserve experience. Sensuous memory was all knowledge to them. And so when literacy and writing came to Kambar, it came as unique excitement, not as routine. Therefore, he builds. He does not, because he cannot, reduce and classify (Taranath).

Kambar was a major figure in the movement of 1960s that tried to correlate the folk and modern. "His *Jokumaraswami* had electrified the theatre with its folk structure. The feudal master, the servant who is the strong male, the women who turn between the two (symbolic of earth) . . . all these had made a vivid impact on Kannada culture" (Akshara 1991) and possibly it "is the most popular amateur play in Kannada. It attracts the imagination of the common audience also" (Datta 1988).

Kambar's contribution and service to folk theatre is commendable. "It is Chandrasekhar Kambar who brought the vital folk element into the Kannada theatre. His depth of imagination made him one of the important playwrights in modern Kannada drama. He achieved a synthesis of modernity in thought and folk style in expression" (Datta 1988). He explored the folk elements thoroughly and brought out their power to transform mundane into extraordinary. The events that seem insignificant gained magnificence through such a treatment. In addition to them, "his most significant contribution to Indian theatre is the use of Bayalata, the folk form of North Karnataka, and the Sangya-Bayalata, a folk play of Karnataka. In his plays, he is concerned with human relation with the beyond" (Dinkgrafe & Dinkgrafe).

In fact, the effort made by Kambar to adopt folk form is more natural rather than cultural. He avers: "I belong geographically to a village, and sociologically to what was considered to be an oppressed, uneducated class. I am, therefore, a folk person simply because I honestly cannot be anything else" (Kambar). He further says in 'Folk Theatre as I See It,' that his first long poem 'Helatena Kela,' was entirely drawn from his 'soil.' He looks at his poem after 25 years and comments that most of his writing "is thematically connected with that long poem." He warns that it does not mean creative bankruptcy rather "the sheer comprehensiveness and opulence of the experience . . . articulate the creative urge of my people. I might make bold to state that the kind of folk medium which made 'Helatena Kela,' possible also made *Jokumaraswami*, and other plays of mine possible" (Kambar). It is the spontaneity of expression that makes his treatment of folk form unique and grand.

Kambar celebrates myth in his plays. In his 'Introduction,' Kirtinath Kurtakoti observes: "Since Kambar uses the theatre of the folk, we have to search time and again for the interconnections between a folktale and a myth. I would say they are similar theoretically, except that a folktale is set in a specific regional milieu." Moreover, "Kambar's plays choose their plots from folktales and myths which address the collective consciousness of a community" (1999). His uniqueness rests on his ability to rework mythology so as to suit the present condition. As he is brought up in the country that treasures mythology and its magnificence, the use of mythology becomes natural to Kambar. Compared to other cultures, Indian culture stands supreme in cherishing mythological events and details. "Behind all the Upanishadic monism, India is mythical. Because we still bargain with our gods and walk among them and sometimes as them, our worship is essentially participatory. . . . In this, we Indians are a mythical people" (Taranath). In 'My Writing,' Kambar proclaims: "I write. In writing I build what I feel. My feelings are my experiences and I build with words, which are stories, pictures, pieces of tales, all of which have been a part of my environment. Indeed, my sense of environment both in time and space, are stories, the fantasies, the images I use. . . . My environment has simply to be mine. In order to make it mine, I have to build it. And in this task, I give a character to my environment and receive a character as a poet. We make each other."

Kambar's sagacious treatment of modernism is quite relevant to the current situation of the world. He "writes at a time when a version of western modernism is the presiding tone in Kannada literature. Indeed, some of his less important writings show a naive anxiety to be 'Contemporary'" (Taranath). He determines to reflect his own tradition through his plays. He guards himself from the influence of a foreign culture and upholds nativity. Kambar unveils his views on modernism:

> I am aware of movements like modernism, with its insistent rejection of everything that is facile and lacking in integrity. I am also aware of the profound influence it has had on some of the excellent writers in contemporary Kannada literature. I think a small part of my own writing shows this influence. Standing at this distance, however, I wonder if the structures of modernism as they have come to us from the West are necessary springs in the task I have of relating with my environment.

The present paper discusses *Sirisampige* which is the complete and intense expression of the dualities of human existence. Written in Yakshagana style, the play improvises on the folktale narrated by A.K. Ramanujan and other stories he had heard in his village. Through the concept of split, the play revolves round the separation of body and soul resulting in dualities tormenting both. The myth of Narcissus is given an innovative treatment lending it multidimensionality. In fact what Narcissus lost on the stage, Sirisampige grabbed it from the audience. Sirisampige is an extension of Kambar's Narcissus. The failure of the powerful but very tough symbolism in Narcissus is transformed into grand success through a very sensational folk story and Yakshagana presentation. The sufferings of incompleteness and the human yearnings towards completeness are reflected in the protagonist Shivanagadeva and others. Bhagavata's prayer introduces the theme of duality. What is a game in the hands of Shiva is a tragedy in human beings. Shiva, the integration of masculine and feminine principles, is at once the symbol of duality and unity. The mythical duality becomes an expression of zeal towards perfection. The tragedy of Shivanagadeva begins with the major tragic flaw--searching a prefect beauty for marriage. The mother's advice in response to the wish, "Which maiden is flawless? Son, if you want such a maiden, then you yourself must be your own wife," (9) foretells the coming tragedy. The lamp maiden that enters his body is the exact concretization of the abstraction of self-love, but the protagonist mistakes this self-love for the love for the maiden and goes in for splitting. From this ritualistic splitting Shivanagadeva splits not only his life but the life of the nearer and dearer ones. The body and the soul get separated and the duality and incompleteness push him to the abyss of death and destruction. The love-hate relationship of Shivanagadeva and Kalinga, Shivanagadeva and Sirisampige is the result of the duality between the body and soul. Through unravelling the psyche of the character, Kambar exposes the tragedy of disintegration. The tragedy of splitting has created a strong illusion in the mind of the prince. The dualities are the destroyers of clarity, conviction and decision. Shivanagadeva's descriptions of his experiences near the pond are used in the analysis to show the confusion regarding his spiritual ecstasy and later the news of Sirisampige's pregnancy transforming the same spiritual ecstasy into a hellish experience where he is eating his own corpse symbolizing the destructive quality of self-love.

The writing throws light on Sirisampige's suffering. Her justification for her immorality echoes the voice of a liberated woman. The boldness and clarity with which she explain the reasons for her immorality challenge the critical comments of few critics who say that Kambar's women characters lack individuality and independence.

The suffering of Shivanagadeva reaches such an extent that he is forced to conclude that body is pure but the soul is sinful. The paper highlights the unique point where the common notion of soul being pure and body impure gets reversed and shattered. It also throws light on the strong influence of conjugal jealousy over narcissism and spiritual glorification. The downfall of mistaken spiritual ecstasy into conjugal jealousy is again the product of the dualities.

The sub-plot of Awali, Jawali and Kamala cannot attain the philosophical height but it parallels the main plot with the same amount of suffering. The physicality of the sub-plot in a way reflects mankind's too much indulgence in physical activities namely love and sex which in turn lead to violence, jealousy, hatred and destruction.

The attempt stresses the suffering of Kalinga also. Shivanagadeva at the end while dying realizes the horrible mistake, and gets the glimpse of the heavenly unity in the eyes of Kalinga. He dies with a warning that his wife should take care of their son so that he does not experience the sin of splitting. Thus Kambar's intense metaphysical probing into the dualities of existence finds a near perfect dramatic expression in Sirisampige.

The most fundamental duality of human existence, namely the duality between life and death has been a great metaphysical concern in human beings. Death as a meaningful framework to human life has been regarded as one of the fundamental truths. It is clear that everything in the human existence must filter through the duality and reality of our consciousness. The complexities of human condition are the thematic concern of Kambar's plays. Mankind is caught in the sticky network of dualities from which it can never escape. These dualities are regarded as strengths and weaknesses in the long journey of human beings towards completeness.

The play begins with Bhagavata's prayer offering salutations to Savalagi Shivalinga. It is a combination of prayer to the almighty and an introduction of the theme. It also differentiates the human misery from god's game indirectly hinting that Shiva, the integration of masculine and feminine principles, is at once the symbol of duality and unity. What is a game in the hands of Shiva is a tragedy in human beings. Duality forms the focal point in many myths. The multiple layers of meanings the play presents make the audience delve deep into the religious philosophy, psychology and fundamentally the human predicament caught in the dualities. The conflict of the dualities reflects these truths.

The king of Shivapura after his death leaves behind Mayavati, his wife and one-year-old Shivanagadeva. Mayavati takes up administration of Shivapura and sees that he is perfectly trained in all aspects. The family god foretells that Shivanagadeva should be married soon after his voice cracks and that he should not see his own reflection in the water. The anxious mother has decided to arrange the marriage of Shivanagadeva with Pushparaja's daughter Sirisampige. Shivanagadeva disagrees as he wants a perfect dame. Mayavati gives him a week's time. If he fails to find one, he should marry Sirisampige. One night Shivanagadeva encounters a lamp maiden coming out of an idol dancing and entering his body. Shivanagadeva is certain that she is the girl whom he wanted to marry. He tells his mother that he has agreed for the marriage on a condition. His body should be split into two equal halves. The parts should be separately kept in two pots and buried in the midst of flowers. The next full moon day the pots should be opened. From one pot comes a handsome Shivanagadeva and from the other comes the pretty damsel with the lamp. A marriage should be arranged between the two, otherwise he will remain a bachelor. With great anxiety and reluctance Mayavati and the elders of the village agree. The ritual as explained by Shivanagadeva is done accurately. But on the full moon day, when the pots are opened, Shivanagadeva comes from one pot and from another comes a king cobra. Completely dejected Shivanagadeva, as per the agreement, marries Sirisampige reluctantly. Shivanagadeva, after the marriage, restlessly disappears as in search of something and returns hopelessly resulting in the sorrow of Sirisampige and his mother Mayavati. Mayavati appoints Jawali to follow the prince and find out where he goes and what he does. They realize that prince Shivanagadeva sits before the lake and pines looking at his own reflection. On the other hand, the cobra Kalinga succeeds in attracting Sirisampige and enticing her towards an extra-marital, immoral relationship.

When the prince comes to know that Sirisampige is pregnant he doubts and forces her to go in for the trial by ordeal. Sirisampige accepts the snake ordeal which involves the test and also the punishment if she proves to be wrong. Naturally she wins the trial as the snake is Kalinga. Later the prince takes out the truth from his wife. The tortures of Shivanagadeva reach the zenith, and he decides to kill Kalinga who has come to see the newborn babe. He escapes in the form of the snake but is killed later. Soon after the death of Kalinga he collapses with severe weakness. After realizing that Kalinga is his own half he sends for Sirisampige and Mayavati to tell the truth. At the end of the play, while dying he advises his wife Sirisampige to take care of the baby so that he doesn't split himself like his father.

The sub-plot which consists of Awali, Jawali and Kamala also faces the same problem of duality. While Shivanagadeva is reluctant to marry Sirisampige, Awali and Jawali are fighting with each other to marry Kamala. When Kamala realizes that both are aspirants, she arranges a fight and decides to marry the winner. Jawali wins and Awali goes to forest. Jawali marries Kamala but cannot consummate his marriage because he feels the presence of Awali everywhere. Kamala laments that she could not win her husband's love. The reappearance of Awali creates confusion. She believes the family god's oracle that she should make a garland of jasmine flowers grown on the anthill and put that garland around her husband's neck. If the ritual is performed, the husband comes in the form of snake and makes love. She follows the advice of her family god. Jawali transforms into a snake and makes love to his wife. But Awali kills the snake and also the eggs of Kamala. Kamala gets wild and plucks her breasts, throws them on Awali and disappears; later Awali also dies as he jumps into water to fight with Jawali looking at the reflection in the water.

Sirisampige, through dramatizing the cruelty and frustration involved in the marital relationship between Shivanagadeva and

Sirisampige, deals with the duality between the material and spiritual, between the body and mind. The main plot and the sub-plot are perfectly grafted to achieve a meaningful unity and philosophic beauty. Though they emerge from different grounds, they complement each other. The main plot reflects a tragic outlook from the beginning of the play. Whereas the sub-plot outwardly reflects the comic and as it progresses it gains the strength of supporting the main plot with its tragic end. They stem from different grounds but unite at the end giving the tragic experiences. One can feel the dualities of tragic and comic overtones in the main plot and the sub-plot. The disintegrating elements finally achieve a kind of integration to give a final meaning to the play. The coordination between the two is a wonderful achievement of Kambar's structural skills.

The love-hate relationship between Awali and Jawali stands as a strong support to the same kind of relationship between Shivanagadeva and Kalinga. The experiences of both the pairs towards oneness though they are not one outwardly are presented in an excellent manner through the confusing network of duality and unity. *Sirisampige* stands as a superb example of Kambar's handling of the theme of dualities of human existence.

The techniques of Yakshagana adopted by Kambar in *Sirisampige* suit the structure and the theme of the play in a natural manner. Bhagavata not only represents the tradition of Yakshagana, he works as a narrator, commentator, singer and an actor also. He becomes an integral part of the play partaking the joys and sorrows of other characters especially those of the clowns Awali and Jawali. The sub-plot which consists of these professional clowns has meaningful organic relationship with the main plot. With their comical foolishness they move parallely to the experiences of the characters in the main plot and gradually unite with it because fundamentally their problems are same, the problems of duality. The prolific use of music, songs sung by chorus, the Bhagavata and the prose compliment the theme and structure. They not only arrest the attentions of the audience, but also attempt to unravel the psyche of the characters. The conflict between the body and the soul is an abstract concept. Kambar gives it a concrete form through the process of splitting the body into two as a kind of an experiment in the play. This inherent desire to reach the difficult and complex world of abstract through not so complex world of concrete is a familiar quality of Kannada writers. D.R. Nagaraj recognizes this when he says that the Kannada mind delves deeply into the concrete. Kambar chooses the folk myth, folktales and other folk models to probe deep into the metaphysics.

Some critics have analyzed the search for the lamp maiden as a mythical expression of the symbolic truth. According to them it symbolizes the prince's search for the transcendental truth or ideal image or spiritual light. The image of lamp is the connotation of spiritual as well as physical light. The fact that Shivanagadeva rejects Sirisampige, who is very pretty, coming from a royal family, shows that the prince is above the mundane world which has hunger for higher truths. His description of the experience near the pond reveals multiple aspects of transcendental experience as codified in all the organized religions of the world. The mythical consciousness always perceives Man-God relationship as a mutual affair. God will not descend to man until man ascends to god. Human beings endeavour to visualize the invisible and reach the spiritual heights. Thus, there is always a balance between desire and satisfaction, quest and fulfillment. Shivanaga's life will be meaningful only when he attains the divine consciousness or spiritual harmony with the absolute. The union between man and god has been viewed as yoga Samadhi. The prince has achieved such a mystical union at the pond. The experience of Shivanagadeva raises many questions. Is the lamp-maid his lover, or his own spirit? If it is just lamp maid the prince's lover, the excessive love for the other may reach the spiritual height leading to mystical experience. Then the above analysis seems reasonable. But if you consider the lamp-maid as the symbol of Shivanaga's self-love, the analysis seems unreasonable, because self-love pushes one to the dark depths of the abyss. There is no spiritual elevation. Shivanaga can mistake and confuse the love for the self as love for the other because he is caught in duality and illusion. But readers and critics need not get caught in the same confusion and duality. Later the prince himself comes and explains his misunderstandings by saying that the reflection was neither God, nor the lamp-maid and was not even his reflection, but the corpse. The tragedy of splitting has created a strong illusion in the mind of the prince. The dualities are the destroyers of clarity, conviction and decision.

There is always a tendency of preferring soul to the body; the same tendency urges us to think that Shivanaga, the representative of mind and soul represents the luminous side of human life. Kalinga represents the dark side of the same. He is obviously a dark god of the nether world. The prince represents the angelic aspects of human life. He belongs to the upper world. Kalinga represents the devilish aspects of human life and belongs to the nether world. So, the duality between the soul and body is also the duality between light and dark, upper world and the nether world and between conscious mind and unconscious mind respectively. The confusing network of multiple dualities in the play gives a mystical and metaphysical outlook to the play. The zeal to understand the mysteries of human life becomes Kambar's main concern.

The mythopoeic qualities of Kambar's plays are strong enough to bear the weight of the abstract metaphysical probing. The folktale narrated by A.K. Ramanujan with variations has been dramatized with Yakshagana technique to present before the literary world the fragrant beauty of Sirisampige. The concept of total theatre as conceptualized by Kambar includes music, dance, action, dialogues not as embellishments, but they are the play. In *Sirisampige*, he uses Yakshagana technique because there are similarities between his total theatre concept and Yakshagana technique. The Bhagavata performs as a grand master, a director controlling the song, action, dance and dialogue.

The use of these techniques is analyzed by Purushottan Bilimale. There is a difference between the way they are used in their original forms and the way they are used by Kambar in his plays. Kambar himself says: "Folk dramatist will become one with his composition. But the modem playwright, because he writes with personal consciousness, there establishes a gap between him and the folk elements. To speak about myself, it is not possible for me to use the folk elements wholly as they are. I use it as a technique for a definite purpose. I make music and dance not as mere embellishments, but to perform a deed, because I write for the Bangalore audience. So I try to turn folk qualities towards various possibilities" (qtd. Bilimale 82).

The compromise between the folk consciousness and the modern consciousness seems inevitable. The critic searches reasons for this in colonial education. It may be true, but we cannot deny the fact that any writer for that matter cannot escape the temporal and spatial influences. In fact they determine a writer's thought process. If duality is an inescapable truth in the life of human beings, there is no problem in accepting the duality in Kambar's literary career also. It is true that the unsplit world that has been internalized by Kambar splits and shatters. But the eternal search of Kambar's poetic consciousness is always towards that completeness and total unified world. The unsplit world of Shivapura is shattered by the onslaughts of modernism. This aspect brings tragic elements in Kambar's world of plenitude and celebration. H.S. Shivaprakash differentiates Bendre's harmony from that of Kambar and says that Bendre's world is a harmonized world blessed by the mercy of Shiva (Shiva Karune). But Kambar's harmonized world is threatened by the cruelties of the colonial onslaughts as a result there is tragic interplay (Rudravilasa). H.S. Shivaprakash's analysis is acceptable but it should have gone a step ahead to realize the fact that the present practicality of world doesn't reflect the mercy of Shiva alone. Kambar tries to reach the Utopian world blessed by Shiva's mercy. But the journey towards that ideal is distracted by the cruelties of time which are inescapable. This tragedy man has to bear because it is of his own making. It is his hubris and his own tragic flaw. Repentance and suffering are the only way to get purged. Kambar's world reflects this search, the tedious journey troubled by fundamental questions of the whereabouts of this catharsis. Shivanagadeva of *Sirisampige* suffers and spreads that suffering to the near and dear ones because of his tragic flaw. His splitting is enforced by his desire to marry a perfect maid. This desire for perfection is also enforced by self-love. This is a truth which he realizes later. The play not only deals with the duality between the body and the soul but also with another problematic human aspiration, i.e. self-love. The myth of Narcissus is also a strong reconstruction in the play. The folktale is modified to suit the purpose of Kambar.

The fact that Kalinga, the cobra came out from another pot is not told to Shivanagadeva. Mayavati and other elders try to give evasive answers and Shivanagadeva is married to Sirisampige as per the agreement. But the obsession of the lamp maid doesn't allow him to love Sirisampige. The same obsession keeps him away from the palace and attracts him towards the woods. In the forest the pool is the point where Shivanagadeva tries to find a kind of satisfaction because the Narcissism that he suffers from comes to the surface as he looks at his reflection. Jawali who has gone there as a spy reports:

Jawali: His reflection came up there like a floating corpse. The moment he saw it, his face shone, tears of happiness came to his eyes. In his ecstasy no word came from his mouth. As if silently talking with that corpse, he sat there, still.

Mother: Strange! And then,

> Jawali: He caught the reflection in his cupped hands and looked at it. The water spilled out between his fingers. Again he caught it and again it spilled. Then, as if the whole forest were crying, he raised his voice saying maiden, maiden and weeping. (VII 27)

Jawali's report of the reflection in the water as a floating corpse is the wonderful imagination of Kambar; too much of self-love leads to total destruction. This truth is reflected in the lines as a kind of warning but Shivanagadeva does not take heed of this warning as he is totally obsessed with lamp maiden, not knowing that she is his own spirit. Shivanagadeva does not realize that he already has in himself what he seeks outside. Shivanagadeva who is buried in self-love does not understand the true nature of the self. This cheating of the self takes place because the story uses a concrete lamp maid for an abstract called self-love. The romantic, love-sick Shivanagadeva can never perceive self-love beyond the lamp maiden. He can never understand the abstract beyond the concrete. Self-acceptance allows access to divinity, longing for it makes it possible. Reaching and touching it causes it to be elusive. One should understand the longing.

Self-knowledge is never a curse, but blind infatuation blocks all the ways leading to self-knowledge. This is what happens in Shivanagadeva. Reflection on the water surface is always illusive, disappears if you touch it. His zealous attempts to hold his reflection which he sees as the lamp maid shows his illusion. He is sure that he is in search of the lamp maid. Self-love in the concretized form of love towards a maid is a wonderful deviation from the myth. In the myth of Narcissus, he spurns and rejects all lovers including Echo and falls in love with himself, not knowing that it is the reflection of his own beauty. Kambar makes Shivanagadeva search for his lover. He is made to see the lamp maid in his own reflection. Love towards the self is mistaken as love towards the other. The duality of the self and the other is the main problem that torments Shivanagadeva. The ambitious egoistic and ruthless pursuit of seeking the lamp maid becomes a character disorder and hence the suffering.

Kambar has tried to reach the abstract through the concrete. But Shivanagadeva fails to understand the abstract which is in the form of the concrete. The lamp maid is a creation of Kambar's genius. The original folktale narrated by A.K. Ramanujan doesn't have the lamp maid. The duality between the abstract and the concrete adds to his other duality of the body and the soul. The amalgamation of the folktale with Narcissus myth is harmonious. Listening to Jawali's report, mother Mayavati is sure of the resulting sorrow. Because the family god's oracle had said that he would become a monk if he saw his own reflection in the water. But instead of becoming a monk, Shivanagadeva is infatuated by the lamp maid. The infatuated and obsessed prince describes in an ecstatic manner the harmony between himself and the reflection, himself and the lamp maid. His description shows the depth of his obsession. The self-indulgence without having the strength of introspection and self-control leads towards self-deception and self-destruction. The whole process with these chain-reactions pushes him towards the total destruction, destroying the near ones also. He does all this in the name of pure love towards the lamp maid. The harmony he describes to Jawali reaches spiritual heights. This glorification of his harmonious love and spiritual experience make us realize how deep he is in the abyss. But he says he has reached the zenith of spirituality. What a difference! This fantastic dramatic irony is a stroke of Kambar's genius. After listening to the prince, Jawali condemns it and tries to make him realize that it is his own reflection, but in vain. Again Kambar makes us realize the irony of the situation. Jawali can make plenty of advice to the prince but he himself cannot come out of that illusion in his life. There are three Narcissuses in the play. All the three, Shivanagadeva, Awali and Jawali, suffer from illusions. They are caught in dualities. The duality begins in their confusion regarding their age. They don't know who is younger and who is elder. Throughout the play they address each other as either younger brother or elder brother. Like yin yang theory, Awali finds an element of himself in Jawali and Jawali also finds an element of himself in Awali. While this is the case with the brothers, Kamala's confusion is also problematic. Kamala's marriage, love, procreation all the three are destroyed because of these dualities. Even god's oracle doesn't solve her problem. The sub-plot with the scenes of Kamala's confusion and sorrow, Awali and Jawali's competition for love, sex, hatred and jealousy show the tragic conditions of human beings who suffer because of these weaknesses and dualities.

Jawali and Awali cannot understand the philosophy of body and soul. They cannot rise up to the level of the prince and his suffering. But they also suffer and get destroyed by their intense competition to win Kamala's love. On the surface, it seems their love, sex, hatred and jealousy are responsible for their tragedy. But the origin of all the weaknesses is in the duality. The physicality of the sub-plot in a way reflects mankind's too much indulgence in physical activities namely love and sex which in turn lead to violence, hatred, jealousy and destruction. Jawali humorously expresses his understanding of the soul through the body: "To me 'body' means an empty stomach and soul means a full stomach. What do you say?" (VII 30)

In contrast to this, the main plot has the touch of spirituality in the very problem of duality. Sirisampige is less tormented by these dualities. While Shivanagadeva spends his life pining before the pool, Sirisampige falls prey to Kalinga's attraction. In the beginning she shows all the signs of chastity and fights back Kalinga's advances, knowing very well that she is losing her self-control. The outward show continues. She declares that her virtue is in her hands. But it doesn't take much time to yield to his attraction.

The speed with which she yields to the sexual attraction of Kalinga reflects the reality of carnal desires of human beings. Once she establishes her illicit relationship, she is not afraid. There is clarity in her mind and expression. She may be suffering, but she knows the reason. Kambar's women characters are quite bold in their sexual ventures and choices. They have always preferred virility. Sirisampige is no exception. She accepts her adultery boldly at the end. If she had been given the chance to explain before the snake ordeal, she would have told the truth. But she doesn't get the right chance. She accepts the snake ordeal because she is quite confident that Kalinga would save her. In the eyes of the people of Shivapura, she becomes an angel as she succeeds in passing the snake ordeal. She expresses her guilt and also her suffering before the prince without any fear or hesitation. She is ready for the punishment also. When the prince condemns her for cheating the elders and townspeople, she says:

> Sampige: That is your ill fortune. My immorality started, my lord. When you forgot the body and began craving for the god, and slipped away from our bed.
>
> Prince: Do you know the punishment for immorality?
>
> Sampige: Was I born for half-men? I was born for and I am seeking the wholeness of the linga of God Shiva. But what fell to my lot was a child born illicitly to an incomplete being. A child born to a widow, you have come here to kill the woman who gave birth to an illegitimate child? Look, I am ready! (XIV 58-59)

The above words of Sirisampige reflect her helplessness, boldness, clarity, suffering and her preparedness to get the punishment. Indirectly she voices her opposition for the prince's behaviour. She reminds him of his failure as a husband. Her questionings echo the voices of many women in search of liberation. Very importantly she comments on the splitting of the prince. She explains how his splitting has split her. She laments how her life's search for completeness ended up in a split. At the end of the scene when the prince goes to kill his enemy Kalinga, Sampige exclaims: "Now I am a complete widow" (XIV 59].

The suffering of Shivanagadeva is intense. The prince who expressed ecstasy at the harmony near the pool has now realized the deception. Now his yearning is of a different kind. The soul needs a body. The abstract needs the concrete. He explains this to Sirisampige. This realization may be partly due to the fact that Sirisampige is pregnant. Probably at this point of time he realizes that he has no body, and it has been stolen by somebody.

Now the question of how and why the prince realized his bodylessness is a significant one. The experience of the prince near the pool, as he himself explained was an engrossing one. The prince had almost forgotten the world around him. But as soon as he realized that Sirisampige is pregnant, he shakes off his numbness and realizes that his body has been stolen. Is this realization a normal, gradual self-realization or an enforced realization which comes through a strong suspicion and conjugal jealousy? The male dominant behaviour is clearly reflected here. The conjugal jealousy questions the violation of the male ownership of the female body. This disturbs his engrossed experience near the pool. The mist of Narcissism melts before this problem. The realization and the reason for the realization, both are worth pondering over. The prince comes and tells his wife that what he saw in the pool was neither a lamp maiden, nor a god and not even his reflection and he was enjoying his own destruction through eating his own dead body. It is not an ordinary enlightenment. The bodylessness becomes a prominent problem because of the conjugal jealousy and suspicion listening to the news of his wife's pregnancy. Shivanagadeva behaves like a true husband now! All of a sudden the authority of a husband is awakened. Though the shrouded mist of Narcissism melts, the problem of the split persists.

The above analysis has a point to prove. Soon after the explanation, not bothering that it is midnight, he quite authoritatively orders for a trial the next morning. The mother and servants are puzzled. Kambar works miracles through this story. The multiple layers of meanings in the play are hidden like a treasure. The treasure hunt is a challenging and exciting task. The male domination starts functioning. The prince tells his wife that body is pure, but the soul is dirty. Sins are visible to the soul.

Kalinga's suffering is of a different kind. Kalinga, the representative of the body enjoys love and sex with Sirisampige but realizes that he too lacks something. He speaks of a dark shadow between them. He says to Sirisampige before the prince tries to search and attack him: "Before, I saw your body. Now I see nothing but the shadow. That shadow is the truth between us, I feel." (XII 55-56)

Kalinga feels lighter after sharing this experience with Sampige. Kalinga and Shivanagadeva experience, a kind of love-hate relationship. The problem of duality peeps here also. The prince explains this to his mother that even his hatred is split into two. He is unable to hate the queen wholly. He is curious to see his other half. He is a confused mixture of admiration, jealousy and half-hatred. The all-powerful split appears and haunts like a ghost with its omnipresence, omnipotence and omniscience. There is an encounter between the two resulting in a battle. Shivanagadeva kills the snake but doesn't feel victorious as he sees the truth in Kalinga's eyes. Shivanagadeva quickly realizes that Kalinga is his body and Sirisampige has not committed the sin of adultery. He also realizes that the whole tragedy began with his splitting. The unity of body and soul, the snake and eagle is reflected in the eyes of Kalinga. Shivanagadeva observes that and explains it to his mother:

> In his eyes the lovely blue sky was reflected. I saw in the sky an eagle and a snake flying together. The snake, which had within it all the dark black secrets of the nether world, was not in the claws of the eagle but was wound around its neck and body in friendship. The duality of the snake and the eagle had been erased and they

> had become one. The mercy of Siva's divine eyes was falling on them in the form of the sun's golden rays. What I saw now was like a snake playing in the sky, opening his hood. Only the snake was visible, having completely taken over the eagle, and it looked as if the snake with its open wood had sprouted wings and was flying. Then that eagle, with its forehead set to the streaming sun, climbed fearlessly into the eternity of the sky. (XVI 65-66)

The conflict between the serpent and the eagle is a popular image appearing in various myths across the world. The serpent is bound to earth and the eagle symbolizes the spiritual flight. The harmony between the two creates the wonderful dragon, a serpent with wings. These images are seen in Polynesian and Egyptian myths.

But in *Sirisampige*, the image is shown in the eyes of the dying Kalinga. The image symbolizes the enlightenment. But the enlightenment occurs at the point of death and destruction. Shivanagadeva and Kalinga reach this enlightenment after destroying their lives. Shivanagadeva after killing Kalinga feels the spine's knot slipping. While dying he requests that the young prince should perform the last rites for both Kalinga and Shivanagadeva. He also advises his wife to take care of the son so that he does not split himself. The play ends with the realization of the grave mistake and caution for the prevention of the same in the future.

The relationship between self-love and self-destruction gets gradually concretized and clear in the play. It also reflects the truth that the splitting of a person into body and soul, not only destroys the completeness but the separated body and soul decay beyond repair. The dualities of human existence haunting Kambar from the beginning have taken the shape of incompleteness in *Sirisampige*. Thus Kambar exploits the mythopoeic symbolic form and successfully gives a dramatic shape to his meditations on the duality of human existence.

The community consciousness with which Kambar enriches his works enables him to concentrate on personal conflicts and also on how these give way to the cultural community conflicts. The myth consciousness of Kambar reflects the contemporary anxieties and at the same time universal truths also. Kambar effectively extracts the symbolic power of the folk myths. His reworking of myths is inspired by the desire to experiment with innovative techniques in theatre; it also reflects the pressure of the community's cultural politics.

Works Cited

Benedict, Ruth, *Patterns of Culture*, Boston, 1944; 1961.

Bilimale, Purshottam. *Kambarara Sahityadalli Jaanapada Tantra*, ed. H.S. Shivaprakash.

Clodd, Edward. *Myths and Dreams*. London, 1891.

Moyers, Bill. "Introduction," *The Power of Myth*, ed. Joseph Campbell, Betty Sue Flowers. New York: Anchor Books, 1988, xii-xiii.

Kambar, Chandrasekhar. *Sirisampige*, trans. Rowena Hill. K.P. Vasudevan.

_____. *Ranganirantara*, Bangalore, 1997. 77-86.

Ramaswamy, N.S. *Sirisampige and Other Plays*. Bangalore: Provoke India, 2009.6-67.

Sauerberg, Lars ole. *Version of the Past-Visions of Future*. London: Macmillan, 1997.

Exile and Displacement of Female Protagonist in Two Folktales of Uttarakhand

DEEPAK BIJALWAN
Res. Sch., H.N.B. Garhwal University, Srinagar

Folktales have always been a part and parcel of any particular community's culture. They have been conveying the ethos of the societies with a detailed picture. This paper discusses two well-known folktales from Uttarakhand: "Rami Bahurani" and "Sadai." The particular angle of discussion will be exile and displacement of female protagonist. Uttarakhand is well-known for its cultural heritage and folk literature. Folktales through their amazing charm and mysterious narrative structure framed the culture of Uttarakhand beautifully. The modern generation is not in touch with this phenomenal school of literature; hence it is a high time to bring to the modern youth the astonishingly crafted beauty of folktales and the ancient ethos of their culture and civilization. Folktales are an important genre of folk literature and represent the feelings and life style of the specific community they come from oral tradition. They are orally conveyed to us from generation to generation. Many folktales of hill region of Uttarakhand are now well documented. Folktales deal with legends, adventures, magic, romance, myth and other aspects of human life and provide a deep understanding of various customs and culture. As a critic puts it: "folklore is concerned with the modes of diversity in our real life and living together, with the nuances that have to be understood in the real-life situations of living together in community." (Ryan 184)

Previously folk literature was known in England as Popular Antiquities. Later in 1846 William John Thomas, a British antiquarian, sent a letter to the Magazine *The Athenaeum* in which he suggested the new word 'Folklore' in place of either Popular Antiquity or Popular Literature. He wrote: "Your pages have so often given evidence of the interest which you take in what we in England designate as Popular Antiquities or Popular Literature (though by-the-by it is more a lore than a Literature, would be more aptly described by a good Saxon compound "Folklore'—lore of the people)—that, I am not without hopes of enlisting your aid in garnering the few ears which are remaining, scattered over that field from which our forefathers might have gathered a goodly crop." (4)

All the available definitions of 'folk' provide us with a significant insight that 'folk' has its identity in mass or group of any size. It may be equal to a nation or may be a few families living in any part of the globe. This kind of literature survives as it represents the beliefs, social patterns, relationships, family structures, economic activities etc. of not just the characters of the folktales/ folklores but of the ordinary people. The importance of folk literature is enhanced by the fact that they represent the life in the region inhabited by the characters and highlight the life of the ordinary people otherwise unsung in history. The folk characters represent the types of the people, not just individuals portrayed in the folktales. As Dorson writes: "The folk literature of a country belongs to its common people whose thoughts and feelings are embedded in it in the most native, down-to-earth and spontaneous way. People since time immemorial have used it to voice or sound their experiences, to throw light on the secret of the physical world and to describe human nature and society. The folktales are deeply rooted in their social environment and are highly sensitive to individual and group sentiments. They are lucid, entertaining, engaging, easily intelligible and memorable. These tales have no fixed form in their oral stage. As long as they are told, they vary, merge and blend. But once they are put on paper, they get stiffened." (59)

Rami, the female protagonist of the folktale "Rami Bahurani," undergoes emotional exile and displacement with dreadful loneliness for twelve years when her husband goes to alien land for job. One day, after a long wait underneath a tree, all of a sudden, he says, "I will leave tomorrow" (160). When Rami shockingly asks him: "Where?" (160), he replies "I will go to *pardesh* and earn money" (160). When he sees the tearful eyes of Rami, he tries to console her and says: "All wives have to bear the absence of their husbands' exile. I will come back soon. It is spring now and I will be returning by the monsoon" (161). Many springs pass but no news about him comes nor does one know where he had gone.

On the one hand Rami's husband undergoes the intolerably distressing feeling of homelessness and restlessness; on the other hand, Rami feels emotionally displaced. Apparently it is her husband who goes away from home but Rami is most affected; she feels insecure and emotionally displaced and looks for her identity as a young married woman. Here emotional displacement does not simply mean getting displaced from a particular place, she floats like a vagabond cloud which makes her feel wasted. She could not free herself from the feeling of displacement, alienation and exile. She creates a fictional world of hope and thinks that she is waiting for her husband. The deep sorrow of her emotional displacement takes away the charm of her youth. Many times she curses her miserable fortune. When she was married at a tender age the womenfolk compared her arrival in her husband's house to the arrival of goddess Parvati to Lord Shiva's abode in Mount Kailash but later on she feels like a poor lady with no life at all: "despite being immersed in the physical work her thoughts kept straying to her husband. She felt terribly lonely even when surrounded by so many family members. For her life was a burden. She felt wasted." (161)

The folktale "Sadai" opens with Sadai's immortal song:

O lofty mountains please bow
O pine trees please bend low.
Far from *maika* this life is full of sorrow
Hope remains to see father's *desh* every morrow.

The bards still sing her songs in the month of *chait* (Chatak 100). The female protagonist Sadai becomes nostalgic about her parents' home and every morning she wishes to see her *maika*. In this folktale, Sadai is married off early to a distant village, all she could see around were tall mountains. The distance between her parents' home and her husband's home is not easily coverable, even the very thought of diminishing this distance to see her *maika* displaces her and she prays to her family goddess for a brother who later on comes to see her. She always misses her *maika* and feels displaced from her roots. Out of her deep sense of displacement and dislocation she planted a *Shilang* plant on a hill top and nursed it with love and affection considering it as her parents' place. She sits near that tree and gloomily expresses her feelings of terrible loneliness and prays to her family goddess Bhawani Maa. Sadai often goes to the tree and cries in anguish, "Alas! If only I had a brother! He would have come for me and taken me home." (100) As a blessing of the goddess, her mother gives birth to a son who one day comes to meet his sister. In this tale the goddess through mysterious ways had tested her faith, devotion, sense of honour, and the spirit of self-sacrifice. It deeply traces out the kind of superstitions and beliefs people had long ago in the hill society of Uttarakhand.

The practice of sacrifice was just a device to test the faith and devotion by mighty powers as it is clear from the translator's preface: "such tales merely represent ancient and medieval belief systems which, like in all other parts of the world, are now extinct from the modern ethos of the hill society." (vi)

It may be concluded that both the tales portray a picture of the culture and customs of Uttarakhand and a glimpse of ancient idealism. The ethical values and aesthetic aspects of the folktales make them universal. We find mention of animal sacrifice in the folktales of Uttarakhand; progressive elements in the society have not only opposed it but also brought reforms in this direction. Folktales have the power to make the modern man realize the fundamental values of human life, rejuvenate their lives and thought processes, and make them experience the bliss of life.

Works Cited

Chatak, Govind. *The Folktales of Uttarakhand*, trans. Arun Pant. Delhi: Jaykay Enterprises, 2015.

Dorson, R.M., ed. *Folklore and Folk life: An Introduction*, Chicago, University of Cairo Press, 1972.

_____, ed. *Folklore in the Modern World*, Paris: The Hague, 1978.

Dundes, Alan. *The Study of Folklore*. Englewood Cliffs, New Jersey: Prentice Hall, 1965.

_____. *Interpreting Folklore*, Bloomington: Indiana University Press, 1980.

_____, ed. *Varia Folklorica*, Mouton Publishers, 1978.

Ryan. http:/www.folklore.ee/folklore/vol46/ryan.

Rama: A Marxist Hero

PINKI ARORA
Research Scholar

Indian folklore has always highlighted bravery. India is a land of rich culture, tradition and heritage. Folk literature binds our rich cultural heritage. Deep-rooted stand our mythological beliefs to which we assign the power to run the world. Indian mythology provides us with such deities who descended on earth to save us from perishing and raise our morale.

Vishnu is believed to sustain the world on his disciple Sheshnaag. Rama, the incarnation of Lord Vishnu, descended on earth to save her from the sufferings given by the demon Ravana. He also taught humanity its lost principles and ethics. Rama, a plethora of love, an absolute who led life in severe perseverance and tolerance with highest moral traits, no matter the hardships he had to face, has the highest seat of love and religion in every temple and is held in high esteem.

The nineteenth century refuted idealism and spiritualism and raised questions about such beliefs. The historical forces arising from a given set of conditions determine the course of action of materialistic men on earth. As Marx says: "In the social production, which men carry on, they enter into definite relations that are indispensable and independent of their will; these relations of production have definite stage of development of their materialistic forces of production. The sumtotal of these relations of production constitutes the economic structure of society, the real foundation on which rises a legal and political superstructure and to which correspond definite forms of social consciousness.

The mode of production of material life determines the social, political and intellectual life processes in general. It is not the consciousness of men that determines their being but on the contrary the social being that determines their consciousness." (1)

Rama descended on earth in Treta Yug to lead the world. One wonders what compelled God to go through the cycle of birth though he could exercise his omnipotence from his heavenly abode. Did he really have to come down and suffer the pains?

Karl Marx wrote in "Oekonomisch-philosophische Manuskripte aus dem Jahre 1844": "the practical production of an objective world, the shaping of inorganic nature is proof of man as a conscious member of the species, that is, as a being who behaves toward the species as towards his own being or toward himself as toward the species. To be sure birds and animals also produce. They build nests and produce for themselves or their offsprings; they produce one-sidedly while man produces universally; they produce only under the domination of immediate physical needs; while man produces independent of physical needs. Animals create only according to the measure and need of the species, while man can produce according to the measure of every species. Hence men also create according to the laws of beauty." (15)

Rama was loved by all his people; but there were his enemies also. Scriptures say that he was incarnated to restore Dharma on Earth. But who were the Demons? Weren't they his creations if he stood as the creator? Then, did the Creator destroy his own creation. Were the Demons an assemblage of only the immoral traits? But who demarcated moral from immoral—we human beings, our society, our social beliefs, which in turn are an offshoot of historical forces. Our social being guided our consciousness of our basic needs and moralities.

It is also said that Rama descended to relieve the Demons from their bodies so that they are reunited with the Almighty. A curse had befallen them for the sins they committed. The Treta

Yug also had the prominent force of territorial expansion where the strong oppressed the weak. Men fought to woo a beautiful rich princess and to succeed the throne. Bravery and strength were strongly sought after.

The class system prevailed and the social picture was more rugged than described by the scriptures. Rama tried to establish an ideal state but himself became a victim of the society. His stepmother had him banished to have her own son crowned. The people of Ayodhya did not welcome Sita when she returned from Sri Lanka. To establish faith and justify his own ideals, Rama abandoned Sita. Even after killing the demons, Rama couldn't give his family a peaceful life. He rescued Ahalaya and fulfilled Shabri's wishes but he himself stood oppressed under the rigid dogmas of society. Rama believed and staunchly supported the welfare of the state. His principles and idealistic philosophy are remarkable. But as Marx said, "we do not set out from what men say, imagine, conceive, nor from men as narrated, thought of, imagined, conceived, in order to arrive at men in the flesh. We set out from real, active men and on the basis of their real life process we demonstrate the development of the ideological and reflexive echoes of this life process. The phantoms formed in the human brain are also, necessarily, sublimates of the material life process, which is empirically verifiable and bound to material premises. Morality, religion, metaphysics, all the rest of ideology and their corresponding forms of consciousness, thus no longer retain the semblance of independence. They have no history, no development but men developing their material production and their material intercourse alter, along with this their real existence the thinking and the products of their thinking." (12)

Work Cited

Marx, Karl and Frederick Engels. *Literature and Art*. International Publishers, New York, 1947.

Oral Stories and Interlinked Characters in the *Ramayana* and the *Mahabharata*

J.R. MEGHANA
Directorate of Distance Education, Kuvempu University

The *Ramayana* and the *Mahabharata* are two great epics of the Indian subcontinent. Over the generations, these have been narrated orally also. Janamejaya, the successor of the Gaurav vamsa (Arjuna's great-grandson) asked the sage to tell the story of his predecessors while he was doing the yagna for snakes. So, Vaisampayana told the story in the presence of the great Sage Vyasa. Vyasa dictated the story and Lord Ganesha wrote it with his tusk. It was in Sanskrit. The stories were written in other Indian languages also. Each Indian language has added some of the incidents according to their culture. So the great epics the *Ramayana* and the *Mahabharata* have many interpolations in them. Though the *Ramayana* and the *Mahabharata* have written editions, still there are many stories in oral literature not yet entered in the written version. This paper aims at describing some of the incidents which are related to the Mahabharata, but are not included in the written literature and remain part of the oral tradition.

The longest-known epic poem, the *Mahabharata*, was not so long once upon a time. It also had humble beginnings—it started out as an orally-transmitted tale of the charioteer bards. But what began as the story of the great Bharata war, ended up being a primer in moral values. By using the dramatic story of the fratricidal war, lessons are given on the four aspects of *purushārtha*, or the meaning of human existence: dharma (law), artha (money), kāma (pleasure) and moksha (liberation).

It was another case of a contradiction between traditional and modern India that was not really a contradiction. While astronomers used advanced instruments to study a solar eclipse this fall, a million ordinary Hindus found a different sort of meaning, travelling to Kurukshetra for ritual baths of purification in a huge lake. Yet for Indian scientists and villagers alike, the northern city of Kurukshetra resonates with historical and spiritual meaning deriving from the stories in the *Mahabharata*, the ancient Hindu epic. It was there, according to the *Mahabharata* that a cataclysmic battle was fought thousands of years ago, drawing in mighty armies from across the subcontinent. The fighting ended in unspeakable sadness, silence and destruction. In New York City, the battle of Kurukshetra is now being portrayed in Peter Brook's sprawling production of "The Mahabharata," which opened Oct. 13 at the Brooklyn Academy of Music. The play marks a rare occasion for an ancient story of the East to be made accessible to modern audiences in the West. The pilgrimage to Kurukshetra for the eclipse indicates that the *Mahabharata* is a living text that permeates contemporary thought and spirit. Its events may have occurred 5,000 years ago. It was probably first written some 2,000 years ago. But its themes continue in the politics, arts and religious culture of today.

"It is said in India that there is nothing in human existence which does not have a place in the *Mahabharata*," said a scholar, Pupul Jayakar, who is the cultural adviser to the Indian Government and impresario of festivals of India in the United States and other countries. "It contains all the contradictions of life, and its legends and stories have been told and retold in every generation."

In the West, the *Mahabharata* has been likened to a combination of the *Iliad* and the *Odyssey*, the Bible, King Arthur's tales and *War and Peace*. Its 110,000 couplets make it the longest epic poem ever written. The actual story, however, makes up only about a fourth of the work. The rest consists of digressions into ethics, philosophy, statecraft, cosmology, myth and countless other subjects.

It is rare to find someone in India who has actually read the *Mahabharata* in original Sanskrit. Educated Indians usually encounter it in any of its hundreds of translations in India's 15 major languages, and many of these translations are considered great works of art.

Modern India is a country in which a lawyer and teacher will tell you with certainty that references to the cosmic weapons used by a hero in the *Mahabharata* intentionally prefigured the space-based Strategic Defence Initiative of President Reagan.

In another conversation, one can hear someone explain how the heritage of the immense ambiguity of the battle at Kurukshetra, which was between two families of cousins, enabled modern India to lead the movement of developing nations professing nonalignment between the superpowers in Moscow and Washington.

At the heart of the *Mahabharata* lies what many scholars feel is the most intense statement of Indian thought ever written, the *Bhagavad-Gita*. In this separate poem, on the eve of battle, the hero, Arjuna, is suddenly paralyzed by uncertainty over the meaninglessness of the war he is fated to fight.

Lord Krishna appears before Arjuna, telling him that life's purpose is a combination of duty and action, even if the consequences seem tragic. Indians of all political persuasions say these lessons sustain them in the political world of today. M.K. Gandhi, the father of independent India, often turned to the Bhagavad-Gita in his moments of great crisis.

Even the most impoverished and illiterate Indian villagers know the stories of the *Mahabharata*, passed on orally by family elders, priests, and travelling bards and minstrels. Along with the other Indian epic, the *Ramayana*, the *Mahabharata* lies at the core of Indian national identity and culture.

One can hardly meet anyone, for example, who has not heard the stories of these epics in childhood from a family member. In India's villages, the popularity of the epics and the ability of people to tell the stories obliterate the Western impression that illiteracy is equivalent of ignorance.

H.Y. Sharada Prasad, press adviser to Prime Minister Rajiv Gandhi, recalled how his own illiterate grandmother could recite and sing passages from the Hindu epics for hours on end. "I remember once she recited 60 stanzas in a row of six lines each, and she told me that she had last recited that passage 60 years before," he said.

Nowadays, especially in the cities, the oral tradition is imperilled. But the epics are being told in different fashions. People buy cassettes of the *Mahabharata* sung in Sanskrit and then translated. Children devour colourful comic-book versions that are the Indian equivalent of the stories of superheroes enjoyed in the United States.

The most popular show on Indian television today is a 52-episode version of the *Ramayana* that features special effects as the hero, Rama, goes forth to rescue his wife, Sita, with the aid of the monkey god, Hanuman. Filming is about to begin on another television serial of the *Mahabharata*.

Other artists draw different parallels. A few years ago, an eminent art film director, Shyam Benegal, produced the movie "Kalyug" about two Bombay industrial houses in combat, with conscious evocations of the fight between the Kaurava and the Pandava families of the ancient epic.

But to many people, the broadest contemporary heritage of the *Mahabharata* is something more ethereal. "At its heart is a certain extremely basic view of life which most Indians hold," said the film and cultural critic Chidananda Das Gupta.

"That is the belief in the transience of life, the questioning of the worth of material things," Mr. Das Gupta explained. "Few other nations have in their background this sense of life's evanescence. At the end of the Mahabharata, everything is gone. All that we collect in life perishes. All that rises like waves eventually falls. All union ends in separation. All life ends in death."

"It sounds trite," he said, "but it pervades the whole of literature to such an extent that there is this link between today's India and India of 3,000 years ago." The *Ramayana* and the *Mahabharata* are two great epics of Indian history about events that took place in entirely different time-periods. While the *Ramayana* happened in Treta Yuga (the second Yuga), the *Mahabharata* is the story of Dwapar Yuga (the third Yuga) having a gap of millions of years. Still to the surprise of many, there were such characters in Indian history that have been a part of both the *Ramayana* and the *Mahabharata*.

Hanuman lifted mountain in the *Ramayana*, he also met Bheem in the *Mahabharata*. Hanuman being the Chiranjivi (blessed with eternal life), is also Bhim's brother, both being sons of Vayu. There is the tale of Hanuman quelling Bhim's pride by appearing as an old monkey when he was on the journey to get the Kadamba flower. Also another tale in the *Mahabharata*, of Hanuman and Arjun having a bet of who was stronger, and Hanuman losing the wager thanks to help of Lord Krishna, due to which he appears on Arjun's flag during the Kurukshetra war. One of the most popular characters of the *Ramayana*, and without his help, Rama may not have found Sita in Ravana's captivity. Or we may say Rama could not have won the battle with Ravana. There is no need to describe the importance of Hanuman in the *Ramayana*. Many claim that Hanuman is still present on earth, somewhere in the Himalayas.

Parshuram's presence graced the *Ramayana* and his curse changed the track of the *Mahabharata*. Parshuram, who appeared in Rama and Sita marriage, is also the Guru of the three greatest warriors of the epic namely: Bhishma, Guru Dronacharya and Karna. Parshuram was in the *Ramayana* when he challenged Lord Rama to break the Shiva Dhanush, which also, in a way, quelled his anger. In the *Mahabharata*, he initially has a duel with Bhishma, when Amba seeks his help in taking revenge, but loses to him. Karna later poses as a Brahmin in order to learn about weapons from Parshuram, before exposing himself, and being cursed by him, that his weapons would fail him when he needed them the most.

Jambavant was the engineer who built the bridge from India to Lanka, who had a duel with Krishna. Jambavant, the bear, is a known and popular character in the *Ramayana*, who was one of the heads in Rama's army to fight the battle with Ravana. He played an active role in Rama's victory against Ravana. He was in the forefront in many instances and was perhaps the only bear in an army of monkeys. Again he has a small role to play in the *Mahabharata*. Veda Vyasa describes vividly all the characters who fought the *Mahabharata* battle for 18 days. But little has been portrayed about the war between Krishna and Jambavant which continued for 28 days in a cave. It was for a Syamantaka mani which Jambavant took from a lion, who got it by killing its possessor. As Krishna was blamed for stealing that mani, Krishna fought Jambavant for that mani to clear his name. Jambavant was defeated and in return offered his daughter Jambvanti for marriage with Krishna.

Mayasura, the father of Mandodari and Ravan's father-in-law, appears in the *Mahabharata* too during the Khandava Dahana incident. Mayasura was the only one to survive the burning of the Khandava forest, and when Krishna finds this out, he lifts his Sudarshan Chakra to kill him. Mayasura, however, rushes to Arjun, who gives him refuge and tells Krishna that he has sworn to protect him. And so as a deal, Mayasura, himself an architect, designs the entire Maya Sabha for the Pandavas.

Agastya was the original possessor of bramhmastra; he met lord Rama before the war with Ravana and gave him the weapon to win the war. The *Mahabharata* also mentions that Agastya was the one who gave the weapon "Brahmashira" to Drona. This was later passed on to Arjuna and Ashwathama.

Kuber was the elder half-brother of Raavan and fund-raiser of Lanka. We all know that Kuber was the wealthiest king alive. It was from him Lord Vishnu took a loan for his marriage and the hundi at Tirupati is supposed to cover the loan and interest amount. In the *Mahabharata*, he was conferred the lord of wealth title by Brahma, as he lost his kingdom in the *Ramayana* to Ravan.

Maharishi Durvasa was the Soothsayer in the *Ramayana*, He went on to test Draupadi and the Pandavas in the *Mahabharata*. Maharishi Durvasa was the one who predicted the separation of Rama and Sita. He also visited the Pandavas during their exile. It is said that it was Durvasa who gave a mantra to Kunti, the mother of eldest three Pandavas for getting children.

Vishwamitra was Ram's mentor. He was also the father of Shakuntala, who is the mother of Bharat after whom the *Mahabharata*, rather the country, is named. That's one long connection.

Narad, one of the greatest rishis, who is well known for gossiping, made his appearance in both the tales. In the *Mahabharata*, he was one of the Rishis who attended Krishna's peace talks in Hastinapur. Well, Narad is the one who inspired Valmiki to write the *Ramayana*.

Vibhishana was another brother of Raavan. He takes the side of Rama during the war. Even though he was crowned the king of Lanka after the war, he knew he would pay the price of betrayal. So in the *Mahabharata* when Yudhistira sent his forces to Lanka, Vibhishana readily accepted the takeover and also sent jewels.

Vashishtha's son Shakti had a son called Parasara and Parasara's son was Veda Vyasa, who wrote the *Mahabharata*. This means Vashishtha was the great-grandfather of Vyasa. Brahmarshi Vashishtha lived from the time of Satyavrata Manu to the time of Sri Rama. Sri Rama was Vashishtha's student.

Vayu Deva was the God of air with two mighty sons, Hanuman and Bheem. Drona's father was Maharishi Bhardwaj, who was the pupil of Valmiki, who wrote the *Ramayana*.

Pulastya was Ravana's grandfather. He is sort of the Moses of Hinduism, because he is considered to have narrated the whole Vishnu Puranam to Parashara.

Atri is a rishi Rama visited. Atri appears before Drona during the *Mahabharata* war. Parshuram and Hanuman are two of the Chiranjivis in Hindu mythology who were granted eternal life and stay in circulation till the beginning of the next *Satyayuga*.

So all the Chiranjivis born before/ during the *Ramayana* are obviously common to both the *Ramayana* and the *Mahabharata*.

Thus, what started out at 10,000 verses in the fifth century B.C., stood at 100,000 verses in the year 400. Yet, the epic continued to be a dynamic text, travelling to various parts of the subcontinent and developing several regional variations. V.S. Sukthankar, a Sanskrit scholar, and his team of scholars began in 1919 the arduous task of preparing a critical edition of the *Mahabharata*. This entailed collecting various manuscripts of the epic and selecting verses common to most versions of the epic. The critical edition ran into 13,000 pages and the project took a total of 47 years to complete. However, the didactic portions of the text are so inextricably linked to the narrative portions, that Sukthankar himself remarked how "useless an exercise it was to reconstruct a fluid text in its original form." The team could, therefore, only reconstruct the oldest known form of the epic, which had been so thoroughly reworked by Brahminical authors that dharma took centre stage and the narrative of the sutras was just the frame. Karna asks Krishna:

> My mother left me the moment I was born. Is it my fault I was born an illegitimate child? I did not get the education from Dronacharya because I was considered a non-Kshatriya. Parshuram taught me but then gave me the curse to forget everything since I was a Kshatriya. A cow was accidentally hit by my arrow & its owner cursed me for no fault of mine. I was disgraced in Draupadi's swayamvar. Even Kunti finally told me the truth only to save her other sons. Whatever I received was through Duryodhana's charity. So how am I wrong in taking his side?

Krishna replies,

> Karna, I was born in a jail. Death was waiting for me even before my birth. The night I was born I was separated from my birth parents. From childhood, you grew up hearing the noise of swords, chariots, horses, bow, and arrows. I got only cow herd's shed, dung and multiple attempts on my life even before I could walk! No army, no education. I could hear people saying I am the reason for all their problems. When all of you were being appreciated for your valour by your teachers, I had not even received any education. I joined gurukul of Rishi Sandipani only at the age of 16. You are married to a girl of your choice. I didn't get the girl I loved & rather ended up marrying those who wanted me or the ones I rescued from demons. I had to move my whole community from the banks of Yamuna to far off seashore, to save them from Jarasandh. I was called a coward for running away. If Duryodhana wins the war you will get a lot of credit. What do I get if Dharmaraj wins the war? Only the blame for the war and all related problems. Remember one thing, Karna. . . . Everybody has challenges in life. Life is not fair on anybody. Duryodhan also has a lot of unfairness in life and so has Yudhistira. But what is Right (Dharma) is known to your Mind (Conscience). . . . No matter how much unfairness we got, how many times we were disgraced, how many times we were denied what was due to us, what is important is how you REACTED at that time. . . Stop whining Karna. Life's unfairness does not give you license to walk the wrong path of Adharma.

There are some tales in the *Mahabharata* which are orally narrated but are not there in written form. Some tales play a prominent role in folk literature. Some of them are upholding Patriarchal Domination; some are focusing Brahminical Values and Upper caste Domination. Some stories are narrated below.

A charioteer's tale. The original story of the Bharata war was probably composed by charioteer-bards known as sutras, who generally accompanied the king's entourage to the battlefield, and composed poems eulogizing their feats in war. These poems were transmitted orally. Several lines in the epic such as, "Eight hundred bejeweled sutras . . . praised him," and "Singers, gāyanas, those skilled in tales . . . dancers and reciters . . . stood praising him, as did the sutras," attest to the fact that the story of the Bharata war was once an orally circulated composition of the sutas.

From the fifth century BC, the Brahmins caught hold of the orally-transmitted poem and committed it to the written word. This was the time when from the numerous chiefdoms, 16 kingdoms were gaining prominence. Two of these kingdoms were Kuru and Panchala, around which the story revolves. Perhaps these emerging kingdoms wanted their history to be recorded? The *Mahabharata* refers to itself as itihāsa. The literal meaning of itihāsa is "thus it was," and has been extended to mean history in the modern age. Thus, the Kuru and Panchala kingdoms treated the Bharata war as their itihāsa and wanted there to be a record of it. The Brahmins, however, could not write the narrative of the bards as it is. Edward Hopkins in his book, *The Great Epic of India: Its Character and Origin,* explained: "The story in its details was so abhorrent to the writers of the epic that they make every effort to whitewash the heroes, at one time explaining that what they did would have been wicked if it had not been done by divinely inspired heroes; at another frankly stating that the heroes did wrong. It is not then probable that had the writers intended to write a moral tale they would have built on such a material. Hence, the tale existed as such before it became the nucleus of a sermon."

Thus, the Brahmins added huge didactic portions in order to explain the "abhorrent details." This explains why the *Mahabharata* as we know it today has two sections—the dramatic narrative and the sermonizing didactic. These didactic sections were inserted into the story at different points of time. Its authors tried to match various parts of the narrative with the Brahminical values prevalent at the time. This constant working and reworking of the text gave rise to several inconsistencies in the narrative. Arjuna's failure to maintain celibacy when sent into exile is one of the most glaring instances. When the Pāndavas lost their kingdom to the Kauravas in a game of dice, they were sent on 13 years of exile, and Arjuna had vowed to remain celibate for the first 12 years. However, Arjuna not only married Ulupi, the beautiful water nymph, but also lived with her for three years. After this, no mention is made of Arjuna's celibacy until Krishna approaches the subject of Subhadra, to which Arjuna replies, "how can a wood wanderer fall in love?" Furthermore, practices, such as Draupadi's polyandry and Bhishma's attempted parricide, which did not have a Brahminical sanction, merited several justifications too.

Drupad, the king of Panchala, organized a competition whereby the man who could string a bow and hit a moving target would win his daughter's hand in marriage. Arjuna, being an ace archer, won the competition and married Draupadi. Yet, Draupadi eventually ended up as the wife of all five Pandavas. This polyandrous alliance merited three different explanations in later additions to the epic:

1. Post Arjuna's marriage to Draupadi, the Pandavas returned to their mother and exclaimed that they had got something for her. Kunti, without even seeing what had been brought to her, ordered that the brothers share whatever had been brought. On seeing Draupadi, Kunti

realized her mistake, but her command could not be violated. Thus, Draupadi is shared by the five brothers.

2. Drupad protested at such an immoral union, but the sage (and also the compiler of the epic) Vyasa explained to him that Pandavas were the reincarnation of Indra, and Draupadi had been reborn as Indra's wife. Thus, their union was acceptable.
3. In another instance, Vyasa explained that a young woman had prayed to Lord Shiva for a husband five times. That woman was reborn as Draupadi, and thus received five husbands, one for each one of her prayers.

Furthermore, the epic stressed that Draupadi's virginity was restored each month (post her menses) so that after willing conjugal sex with one of the Pandavas, she could be a virgin for the next Pandava. A host of explanations were thus offered by the epic's authors with the idea that Draupadi's polyandry was an aberration.

However, Wendy Doniger, in her book, *The Hindus*, points out that Draupadi's was not the only polyandrous marriage. Several other polyandrous unions exist in the epic: Satyawati (two partners, Shantanu and Vyasa's father), Ambika as well as Ambalika (Vichitravirya and Vyasa), Kunti (Pandu, Surya, Dharma, Vayu, and Indra) and finally Madri (Pandu and the two Ashwins). These polyandrous unions point to the fact that when the charioteer bards versified the Bharata war, polyandry was the custom as it is even now in parts of the Himalayas. But when the epic was being written, polyandry had lost Brahminical sanction. Similarly, Draupadi's chastity was stressed upon so as to avoid Sankara (literally, mixing; in this context, mixing of patrilineage), a word that is also used for the deplorable mixing of varnas, or varnasankara. Draupadi's polyandry being central to the narrative of the epic could not be weeded out. Hence, several explanations were offered to explain it.

Between 200 BC and 200 AD, the *Bhagavad Gita*, a huge didactic text (providing justifications for fratricide, among other things) was added to the epic. This was a time when the Puranas were being written and Vaishnavism was becoming popular. Apart from replacing the expensive Vedic yajnas with the simple Puranic pūja, the Puranas also carried out a process of assimilating several deities of the low tradition with the deities of the high tradition. One such deity of the "low tradition" was Krishna, of the Vrishni tribe. Like other deities of the "low tradition" like Jagannath of Puri, Krishna was made one of Vishnu's 10 avatars. Krishna's cult grew quickly and as a result, he was made a central figure in the epic. Similarly, between 200 and 400 AD, didactic sections akin to the *Manusmriti* were also added. This is when Dharma becomes a central concept in the epic.

King Dashratha had a child before Rama and his brothers were born. King Dashratha and his first wife Kaushalya had a daughter named Shanta. Kaushalya's elder sister Vershini and her husband Raja Rompad (who was a great friend of Raja Dashratha as they studied in the same Ashram) had no offspring. Once, when Vershini was in Ayodhya, she joked around asking for a child, to which Dashratha promised her she can adopt his daughter, Shanta. As the promise of 'Raghukul' had to be kept, Shanta was adopted by Raja Rompad, the king of Angdesh.

One fine day, when Shanta had grown to be a beautiful woman, she was in a conversation with Raja Rompad. At this time, a Brahmin came to visit King Rompad requesting help for cultivation during the monsoon. Busy in the conversation with his adopted daughter Shanta, Raja Rompad ignored the Brahmin who left the kingdom. Lord Indra, the God of rains, was offended because a Brahmin devotee of his was insulted. Lord Indra decided to punish Rompad and hence, it did not rain in the coming monsoon.

To get free from this curse, Raja Rompad called Rishi Rishyasringa to perform a Yagna for rains. To honour the Rishi,

King Dashratha and King Rompad decided to marry-off Shanta to Rishyasringa. As Dashratha had no heir yet, he then called Rishyasringa to perform a Yagna for him too, after which the God of Fire gave a dessert to Dashratha for his wives to consume, eating which Rama and his brothers were born.

Rama is considered the reincarnation of Vishnu, Bharat and Shatrughan are considered to be his Sudarshan-Chakra and Conch-Shell, while Laxman is considered to be his Sheshnaag, Vishnu's seat in Vaikunth (abode of Vishnu or Brahmalok). As earth rests on Sheshnaag's head, whenever Adi Shesh is angered, the earth shakes. When in the courtroom of Janak (father of Sita), during Sita's 'swayamvar,' nobody could lift the bow of Shiva, Janak got upset and declared that the earth is now devoid of strong men. This angered Laxman so much that the earth started to tremble. Laxman was later born as Balram, the elder brother of Lord Krishna. Laxman had complained that since he is born as the younger brother, he has to obey all commands of Rama and thus, his wish to be the elder brother was fulfilled when he was born as Balram.

A promise of Rama became the cause of Laxman's death. After Sita was consumed by Mother Earth, Rama knew that his duties on earth were over and he decided to return back to Vaikunth, but that couldn't be accomplished as Hanuman won't allow *Yam,* the God of Death, to meet Ram. To distract Hanuman, Rama threw his ring in the underworld (*Paatal*) and asked Hanuman to procure it. Rama then invited Yam, but he put forth a condition that the conversation between them must remain unrevealed and if anyone intercepts the conversation, Rama would kill the person. Rama asked Laxman to guard the gate to ensure no one came in to intercept the meeting of Lord Rama and Yam. In the meantime, angry sage Durvasa came in to meet Rama only to be stopped by Laxman. Angry Durvasa warned that he would curse Ayodhya if he is not allowed to meet Lord Ram. Seeing the situation, Laxman decided to go and talk to

Rama and hence intercepted the meeting. After this incident, to fulfill his brother's promise, Laxman went to Saryu and gave up his life. Laxman's death before Ram's was necessary as the Sheshnaag (the seat of Vishnu) that was Laxman had to return first before Vishnu returned to Vaikunth. Vishnu here was Lord Ram.

Bali of the *Ramayana* became the reason for the death of Lord Krishna from the *Mahabharata*! Bali, the elder brother of Sugreev, known for his strength, had a boon that whosoever engaged in a combat with him would lose half of his strength to Bali. Invincible Bali was challenged once by Ravan for a combat. Enraged Bali grabbed Ravan by his head and took him around the world, making Ravan accept his defeat. When Bali took over Sugreev's wife and the kingdom of Kishkindha forcefully, Sugreev fled the kingdom and met Hanuman in the woods for help. In the interim, Rama killed a demon named Kadamb in the forest while searching for Sita and the curse-free Kadamb now asked Rama to meet Sugreev to save him from Bali. Rama decided to execute Bali after meeting Sugreev. Rama shot Bali from behind the tree, and Bali alleged that Rama had betrayed him as he didn't challenge Bali for a combat. To this, Rama explained that if a man ill-treats a woman, it is the duty of a righteous man to punish him. Rama then promised Bali that in his next life, he would become the reason of Vishnu's death and thus take revenge for this incident. Bali was later reborn as Jara, the hunter, who was the reason of Krishna's death in the Dwapar Yug!

It is interesting to note that the first letter of every 1000th Shloka of the *Ramayana* together makes up the Gayatri Mantra, making this revered mantra the essence of the epic. There are 24 letters in the Gayatri Mantra and there are 24,000 Shlokas in the Valmiki *Ramayana*. While the Gayatri Mantra has been actually first mentioned in the Rig Veda, it has gained significance, thanks to the *Ramayana*.

Hiranyaksha, Hiraeyakasipu; Ravana, Kumbhakarana; and Sisupala, Dantavakara—all were reincarnations of brothers Vijaya and Jaya, who were at once the gatekeepers of Lord Vishnu's abode!

There is a story in the *Mahabharata* which connects the three epics, the *Mahabharata*, the *Ramayana*, and the *Bhakt Prahlad* in a wonderful way.

According to this story, once, Vijaya and Jaya, the gatekeepers of Lord Vishnu's abode (Vaikunth Lok) were cursed by the four Kumars of Brahma when the latter were mistaken for being children (*Kumars* looked like children due to the strength of their *tapas*!) and were not allowed to meet Narayana. In accordance with the curse, the gatekeepers had to give up their divinity and live as mortals on earth. The news of the curse fell on Narayana's ears, and he felt sorry for his gatekeepers. He also apologized to the Kumars and assured Jaya and Vijaya that he will do something to reciprocate.

Narayana put forth two options: they could either be born seven times as His devotees or three times as His enemies on earth. Since seven lives was a greater time span, which the two brothers could not bear, they chose the latter. In the first birth as an enemy to Vishnu, they were born as Hiranyaksha and Hiraeyakasipu who were killed by Varaha and Narasimha (both avatars of Vishnu). In the Treta Yuga, the two brothers were born as Ravana and Kumbhakarana and were killed by Rama, an avatar of Vishnu. In the Dwapar Yuga, the brothers were born as Shishupal and Dantavakra and were killed by Krishna, an avatar of Vishnu. Hence, with each life, they moved closer to their God.

Duryodhana's real name was Suyodhana. And the rest of the clan was Sushaasana, Suchala and so on and not the Dushasana, Dusshala etc. that we are familiar with. They were all given nicknames to suit their bad reputation. The details are available in a flashback. Long before the *Mahabharata* war, Pandavas were living in exile in a forest. Duryodhana placed his camp on the opposite side of the pond where Pandavas were staying. Once while Duryodhana was taking bath in that pond, the heavenly Gandharvas came down. Duryodhana picked up a fight with them but was defeated and captured. Arjuna saved Duryodhana and set him free. Duryodhana was ashamed but, being a Kshatriya, he told Arjuna to ask for a boon. Arjuna replied that he would ask for the honour gift later when he needed it.

There is a reason why Duryodhana did not participate in Draupadi's swayamvar. It's because he was already married to the princess of Kalinga, Bhanumati. He had promised her that he would never marry another, and he kept his word.

Draupadi's brother was actually a reincarnation of Eklavya. Originally born to Vasudev's brother Devashrava (which by the way makes him Krishna's cousin!), Eklavya got lost in the forest and was subsequently brought up by the Nishad king Hiranyadhanu. He was killed by Krishna during Rukmini's abduction. However, to honour the great sacrifice Eklavya made as *guru dakshina*, Krishna blessed him so that he can reincarnate and take revenge on Drona. Hence, Eklavya was reincarnated as Draupadi's twin Dhrishtadyumna.

Arjuna asked for his gift during that night of the *Mahabharata* war when Krishna told Arjuna of his unsatisfied boon and asked him to go to Duryodhana and ask for 5 golden arrows. When Arjuna asked for the arrows, Duryodhana was shocked but being a Kshatriya, he had to honour his words. Duryodhana went to Bhisma and requested for another five golden arrows. To this, Bhisma laughed and replied that is not possible.

The *Mahabharata* also has the first test tube baby. On seeing Rishi Bhardwaj, the beautiful Apsara Krithaji got out of the Ganga river wearing a single loincloth. Rishi Bhardwaj was moved by the heavenly beauty of the Apsara. Overpowered by the moment, the sage involuntarily emitted his semen. The Rishi collected this sperm in a clay pot and stored it in a dark place in his Ashram. Drona was born in this pot. 'Dronam' means pot and 'Dronar' is one who was born from the pot.

Bhishma was the only legitimate heir to the throne. Let's rewind the story a little bit. First, there was King Shantanu, who married Ganga, who gave birth to eight sons (who were all actually Devas cursed to be born on earth). So Ganga managed to kill the first seven, freeing them from their curse. King Shantanu intervened as she was about to kill the eighth one, saving the only remaining son, whom we know as Bhishma.

The author of the *Mahabharata* is also a character in the epic! We all know that there was no *one* writer who put the *Mahabharata* together. But as per the story, Satyavati had a son with Sage Parashar before her marriage to King Shantanu. Before diving into the sage's advances, Satyavati exacted three wishes out of him; one of which was that the son born of their union be famous as a great sage. Soon after, Satyavati gave birth on an island in the Yamuna. This son was called Krishna-Dwaipayana, later known as Vyasa, compiler of the Vedas and author of the *Puranas* and the *Mahabharata.* He also fathered Dhritarashtra and Pandu. Bhishma pledged that he will never have children. Now here's the thing, Satyavati's two sons with Shantanu died too early. So, Satyavati was left with their two childless widows, Bhishma, and an empty throne. Solution? Satyavati called her other son Vyasa, the same Krishna-Dwaipayana-Vyasa who wrote the *Mahabharata* to impregnate her two widowed daughters-in-law. Ambika gave birth to Dhritarashtra, and Ambalika gave birth to Pandu.

Draupadi was, in fact, goddess Durga's avatar. Once, Bhima saw Yudhistira washing Draupadi's feet in her chambers, and complained to Krishna, not knowing that Draupadi was actually goddess Durga's avatar. Krishna took him to the jungle and asked him to sit quietly on a treetop and witness what happens below. Late in the night, Bhima saw that Draupadi, as goddess Durga, was asking for Bhima's blood in her empty bowl, since he had entered her chambers despite being forbidden from entering. Bhima, scared to death, narrated the entire story to his mother, Kunti. Kunti then asked Draupadi never to hurt Bhima. Being a mortal, Draupadi had to promise her and in the act, she bit her lip hesitantly. Kunti wiped off the blood from her lips with the edge of her cloth and promised her that Bhima will fill the bowl for her. This did happen when Bhima killed Dushasan for humiliating Draupadi and filled her bowl with the blood from Dushasan's chest.

One of the Pandavas already knew that the war will commence soon. Pandu's dying wish was that his sons should eat his brain after his death to gain knowledge and experiences. Sahadev devoured three pieces and became the greatest astrologer, who could foresee events. But he could not tell anyone about the war, because it would bring about his death.

Shakuni, Dhritarashtra's brother-in-law, became the reason of his downfall. Dhritarashtra's wife Gandhari had been cursed that her first husband would die, which led to her family secretly getting her married to a goat, and later killing it. She then married Dhritarashtra. When he got to know about this several years later, Dhritarashtra put the entire Gandhara family, King Subala and his hundred own sons in prison to die. They were only given a bowl of rice to eat. King Subala, who wanted to take revenge on Dhritrashtra, advised everyone in prison to give their food to his youngest son, Shakuni so that he becomes strong enough to fight Dhritarashtra. He also convinced Dhritarashtra that Shakuni can be a guide for his hundred sons, thus asking him to release Shakuni. Before dying, Subala asked Shakuni to make a dice from his backbone with such powerful magic that it could spin the requested number; he also broke one of Shakuni's bones from the leg so that it reminds him of the pain his family went through before dying. And this is how Shakuni became the reason for Dhritarashtra and his dynasty's downfall.

Sahadev who had eaten the brain of his father Pandu after his death could see not only the past and future but also had a great knowledge in Astrology. This is the reason why Shakuni sent Duryodhana to Sahadev to ask the right time (mahurat) for the Mahabharata war. Sahadev being honest disclosed it to Duryodhan in spite of the fact that Duryodhan was his real enemy in the battle.

Balrama was Abhimanyu's father-in-law. Abhimanyu's wife Vatsala was the daughter of Balrama. Balrama wanted that Vatsala should marry Laxman, Duryodhana's son. Abhimanyu and Vatsala both loved each other and wanted to get married. Abhimanyu took the help of his brother Ghatotkach (a daitya) who tricked Laxman and terrified him. Ghatotkach then flew away with Vatsala and went to his brother Abhimanyu. Laxman was very upset at all this and he vowed that he will not marry throughout his life.

Iravan, the son of Arjun and naga princess Ulupi, sacrificed himself to goddess Kali to ensure the victory of his father and his team in the Kurukshetra war. He, however, had a last wish—he wanted to marry a girl before he died. Now, getting a girl who knew her husband would die in a few days was a tricky task. So, Lord Krishna took the form of Mohini, married Iravan and even wept like a widow after her husband died.

Duryodhana had many dilemmas. Lying in the battlefield, awaiting death, badly bruised by the wounds inflicted by Bhima, he kept his three fingers in a raised position and was unable to speak. All the efforts made by his men to understand the meaning proved to be futile. Seeing his plight Krishna approached him and said: "I know what issues occupied your mind. I will address them." On hearing this, Duryodhana closed all the fingers and within seconds he died.

Nakul can drive his horse even in heavy rain without getting wet. He travels with such a speed between a drop and another drop, without getting wet. Only Nakul can do this among Kaurav and Pandav warriors. It also seems that if Yudhistira gets angry, everything that falls within the range of his eyesight will be burnt. This is why Yudhistira was never angry with anyone.

When Karna was lying on the battlefield gasping for breath in his last moments, Krishna assumed the form of an indigent Brahmin and approached him wanting to test his generosity. Krishna exclaimed: "Karna! Karna!" Karna asked him: "Who are you, Sir?" Krishna (as the poor Brahmin) replied: "For a long time I have been hearing about your reputation as a charitable person. Today I came to ask you for a gift." "Certainly, I shall give you whatever you want," replied Karna. Krishna asked for gold: "I want a small quantity of gold." Karna opened his mouth, showed the gold fillings for his teeth and said: "I shall give this to you. You can take them." Assuming a tone of revulsion, Krishna said: "Do you expect me to break your teeth and take the gold from them? How can I do such a wicked deed?" Karna picked up a stone, knocked out his teeth and offered them to the "Brahmin." Krishna in his guise as Brahmin wanted to test Karna further. "What? Are you giving me as gift teeth dripping with blood? I cannot accept this. I am leaving," he said. Karna pleaded: "Swami, please wait." Even while he was unable to move, Karna took out his arrow and aimed it at the sky. Immediately rain dropped from the clouds. Cleaning the teeth with the rainwater, Karna offered the teeth with both his hands. Karna asked: "Who are you, Sir"? Krishna said: "I am Krishna. I admire your spirit of sacrifice. In any circumstance, you have never given up your spirit of sacrifice. Ask me what you want." Beholding Krishna's beauteous form, Karna said with folded hands: "Krishna! To have the vision of the Lord before one's passing is the goal of human existence. You came to me and blessed me with your form. This is enough for me. I offer my salutations to you."

Here is a funny story from oral tradition of the *Ramayana* which is popular in North India and makes us realize the warmth of love between Rama and Hanuman. Hanuman used to complete every task of Rama so quickly and efficiently that no one else got the opportunity to serve Rama. Soon, the family of Rama, especially his brothers, got annoyed that they were not getting the opportunity to serve their elder brother, the royal servants were unable to serve their King and Sita was unable to do any task for her husband. So, everyone, one day gathered and prepared a list of tasks they would do for Ram, starting from the break of day till he slept. Ram's various tasks were divided into time and people so that everyone would get the leisure of serving Ram. But this time Hanuman was not included in the list. He was assigned no chore of Ram.

Suddenly he beamed like a child and realized everyone had forgotten to include one thing to the list which was snapping the fingers (chutki) whenever Rama yawned to avoid entering malevolent spirits in his body (just a folk belief). From then, he used to watch Rama carefully and if he noticed whenever Rama was about to yawn, he ran to him and snapped his fingers. He was always focused as Rama could yawn at any instant. He made sure his one hand was always free to click the fingers. This irked the peoples of the palace.

At night, Rama went inside his bedroom to sleep. Hanuman came too and sat beside his bed. Sita was not amused. She ordered him to go out and let her and Rama sleep in private. So he stood outside and thought that how would he know if Rama was yawning? He could not go inside his private chamber. So he came up with a brilliant plan. He thought to continuously snap his fingers till the sun rose. This way, even if Rama yawned in the middle of the night, his purpose would be served. Rama was about to sleep when he heard the snappings. How could a God waste the efforts of his devotees? So every time Hanuman snapped his fingers, Rama yawned forcefully. Just because Hanuman was clicking his fingers, Rama felt obliged to respect the task of his devotee. This continued for the whole night and Rama kept on yawing instead of sleeping!! Sita was terrified to see what had struck her husband? Vashishtha was summoned and the palace was awake. Their King was struck by some spirit? Vashishtha came and checked Ram. He heard the snappings too and caught Hanuman outside Ram's room at a corner. Suddenly everyone realized what was happening and laughed to his or her heart's content. They made Hanuman see the condition of Rama and requested him to stop. Only when the snapping stopped, Rama relaxed his mouth! No one can separate Hanuman from Rama and Rama from Hanuman. The devotion of devotee makes even the God helpless.

At the end of the war, when Lord Rama asked Jambavan (Jambavant) for a boon, Jambavan asked him to marry his daughter Jambavati. But in that incarnation, Lord Rama had sworn to take only one wife and that was Sita. He, therefore, promised him to fulfill his wishes in his next incarnation as Krishna and also told him that his daughter would retain her youth until then.

In Dwapar Yuga, another girl who was pining of love for Krishna was Satyabhama, the only daughter of Yadava chief Satrajit. Satrajit once had done severe Tapasya to the sun-god Surya, who had given him a beautiful jewel the Syamantaka. This gem had the ability to produce eight times its weight in gold daily if it was worshipped with proper rites. Needless to say, Satrajit prospered, but too much wealth has its ill effects. He started to lapse from the high code of dharma and started living a life of vain and useless luxury. In order to save him, Krishna requested that he hand over the jewel to Ugrasena, the king, but Satrajit refused. He worshipped it daily. The love and devotion that should be given to the god was given to the jewel. He suspected that everyone is after his jewel especially Krishna. One day, his brother Prasena came to him and begged to be allowed to wear the jewel when he went out hunting. Satrajit tried to dissuade him from this foolish act but Prasena didn't give in. At last, he acceded to his younger brother's wish. During the course of the day, Prasena became separated from his companions and found himself alone in the middle of the forest. Suddenly, a hungry lion attacked Prasena and killed him and made off with the jewel. In turn, it was attacked and killed by Jambavan (Jambvanta), king of the bears, who took possession of the jewel and presented it to his daughter Jambavati.

When the hunting party returned without his brother, Satrajit was sunk in gloom and came to the conclusion that his brother had been killed by Krishna in order to get Syamantaka. The rumour soon reached Krishna's ears, he laughed and shrugged it off, but both Balrama and Uddhava insisted that he do something to clear his name. So, accompanied by them and some of the other Yadavas, he set out for that forest. Penetrating deep into the wood, they came across the decomposing body of Prasena. Following the lion's tracks, they climbed up the mountain where they found the carcass of the lion. Not finding the jewel, they followed the footprints of the bear which took them to Jambavan's cave. Krishna decided to step in and forbade anyone else to accompany him and told Uddhava and Balrama to return to Dwarka if he wouldn't appear within 12 days.

As Krishna entered the cave, he found it lit up by the presence of Syamantaka, with which the girl was playing. When she saw the stranger, she ran to call her aged father. Since Jambavan lived alone in the forest with his daughter, his usual method of greeting strangers was to hit first and ask questions later. He didn't recognize that this stranger is none other than his Lord Rama who had now taken the form of Krishna and greeted Krishna with his powerful blows. There was a great fight between them, which lasted 28 days without stopping. Jambavan was the strongest living entity at that time, so he expected to defeat Krishna. After 28 days, Jambavan had perspiration all over his body and was extremely tired. He realized that the person he was fighting must be the Supreme Lord, who is the source of all strength and all kinds of opulence. He offered prayers to Lord Krishna, and hearing of the Lord's desire, he gave him the Syamantaka jewel. He then presented his daughter, Jambavati, to be married to Lord Krishna. Lord Krishna then out of his mercy to his dear-devotee showed his form of Lord Rama.

When Krishna returned to Dwarka with Jambavati and the jewel, he summoned Satrajit to the Yadava assembly, he gave him the jewel and also explained to him how it had been traced. Later, to erase the guilt, Satrajit's daughter whispered to her father that the best way is to emulate Jambavan's example. He went straightway to Krishna and offered him both, his daughter and the jewel. Krishna accepted the former but refused the latter and told him that it is better to let it remain in the temple and every one will derive benefit from the jewel. Rukmani and Satyabhama are supposed to be the incarnations of Goddess Lakshmi and Bhumi Devi (Goddess of Earth).

Five thousand years ago, the Kurukshetra war, between the Pandavas and the Kauravas, was the mother of all battles. All the kings—hundreds of them—aligned themselves on one side or the other. The king of Udupi, however, chose to remain neutral. He spoke to Krishna and said, 'Those who fight battles have to eat. I will be the caterer for this battle.'

The battle lasted 18 days, and every day, a thousand soldiers died. So the Udupi king had to cook that much less food, otherwise, it would go waste. The amazing thing was that every day, the food was exactly enough for all the soldiers and no food was wasted. After a few days, people were amazed, 'How is he managing to cook the exact amount of food!' No one could know how many people had died on any given day.

When someone asked the kind of Udupi, 'How do you manage this?' the king replied, 'Every night I go to Krishna's tent. Krishna likes to eat boiled groundnuts in the night so I peel them and keep them in a bowl. After he is done I count how many nuts has he eaten. If it's 10 peanuts, I know tomorrow 10,000 people will be dead. So the next day when I cook lunch, I cook for 10,000 people less. Many of the Udupi people are caterers even today.

The Govardhan Parvat, situated near Mathura, carries a great religious significance across the country. It is said that doing a Govardhan Parikrama will help you get rid of all your problems. But according to legend, the hill is decreasing in size due to an ancient curse. Though not visible, the hill is apparently decreasing by the size of a mustard seed every day due to a curse by Rishi Pulatsya.

The story goes that Lord Vishnu took the birth of Krishna to eradicate all the evil from the world. Around that time, the Govardhan hill & the river Yamuna also came to the Earth by reincarnating as Dronakala's son (who was the king of mountains). Around that time, Rishi Pulatsya requested Dronakala that he too wanted to take his son from Mathura to Kashi. He was given permission but only on one condition. He would carry Govardhan and would not keep him down till Kashi arrived. The Rishi agreed and the journey started.

On the way, the Rishi passed Braj Mandala lush green pasture which was frequented by Lord Krishna. Govardhan wanted to feel the presence of Krishna there and became purposely heavy. Tired, the Rishi had to keep him down. However, soon the Rishi realized that Govardhan has tricked him. He got angry and cursed the hill that it will decrease by the size of a mustard seed every day and will eventually vanish!

It is also said that till the time the Govardhan hill and the Yamuna river is present on earth, the earth is safe and once they vanish, the earth too will be destroyed!

Much like Draupadi's polyandry, Bhishma's parricide evoked much censure from many authors of the *Mahabharata*. Accordingly, a chain of parricides was constructed in order to justify this ghastly act. Bhishma had tried to kill his preceptor, or guru, Rama Jamadagnya, also known as Parasuram. Since one's preceptor is equivalent to one's father, the act was one of attempted parricide. In order to expiate for his sins, Bhishma then has to be the voluntary victim of an attempted parricide by his grandson, Arjuna. Counselled by his wife, Ulupi, Arjuna decides to pay for his sin by being the victim of an attempted parricide by his son Babhruvahana.

In order to censure one parricidal act, the Brahminical authors of the epic constructed two others not only to show parricide as a sinful act but also to convey the message of karma—one reaps what one sows. Similarly, for the fratricide that lies at the heart of the epic (Pandavas and Kauravas were brothers), a sermon on dharma and performance of caste duties was added as a didactic section.

For Drudarastra, there were 32 plates full of meals that were served each time he ate. That was because he had a curse that if he touched the food on the plate more than once, the food would turn into worms. For a person, 32 handfuls of food are necessary to fill the stomach. So from each plate, Drudarastra took one handful of food and in that manner, he took from 32 plates 32 handfuls and ate. Karna, the eldest son of Kunti was brought up by the chariot driver of Drudarastra. Since Drudarastra's bungalow was the chariot driver's workplace, he used to bring his son Karna there. One day Karna was crawling; he went near Drudarastra's plate. That time Drurastra had taken one handful from that plate. Karna touched the food. Immediately the worms in the plate disappeared. This amazing incident was informed to Drudarastra. Drudarastra felt very happy, picked up Karna, hugged him and praised him saying, "you are the one who came to remove thousands of worms from my food, so you are Karna from today." Karna's original name was Vasusena, and that became secondary, while Karna became his first name. So Drudarastra had a soft corner for Karna. That was why he never controlled Karna's habit of giving away his wealth to all. Karna gave donations from the treasury of Drudarastra. But after

Karna's alms-giving, Drudastra with some disgust used to search the treasury to see whether anything was left there or not. Instead of being empty, the treasury became full.

This episode is not found in the written editions of the *Mahabharata* either in Tamil or Telugu. But it was orally narrated by parents to children. Just like this one, many interpolations are still in oral form and not put into written form. Here are some of them mentioned in the following paragraphs.

Shakuni was the paternal uncle to Duryodhana and younger brother of Gandhari. But he was always trying to ruin the Gaurav dynasty. There was a reason for this. Those days Bhisma was a great warrior. No one could defeat him. If he wanted to do anything, by hook or crook he would do it. He wanted to bring Gandhari as a wife to Drudarastra and a daughter-in-law to his dynasty. But the Gandhara king Supalan did not wish to give his daughter to the blind king. So Bhisma went with his army to conquer Gandhara. Bhisma conquered Gandhara and took the king and his sons as captives. He made Gandhari his brother's wife. Supalan wanted to take revenge on the Gaurav Dynasty; there were a hundred sons. Shakuni was one among them. He was clever and intelligent. In the prison, the jailor used to give a handful of rice to each one of them. Supalan told his other sons that they should give their food to Shakuni, so he could live long and take revenge on Gaurav dynasty. All accepted that suggestion. After some time all the brothers and Supalan died. Shakuni came out of prison and lived with his sister. From that time he began to try to ruin the Gaurav dynasty.

During a gambling game, the Pandavas lost all their property and kingdom. Duryodhana ordered them to go to the jungle for 12 years and follow for a year life incognito, ignoring his father Drudarastra's wish to give back to the Pandavas their kingdom. While living in the forest, whenever they moved from one place to another, they kept moving in one order. Dharma used to lead, behind him came Draupadi, one side of Draupadi walked Bhima, another side of Draupadi was Nakul, behind Draupadi, Arjuna and Sahadev. One day they were walking in the forest. That time a Gandharva was travelling in the sky. He saw Draupadi and was attracted by her beauty. While flying close, he abducted Draupadi. As soon as he heard of this incident, Dharma asked where Draupadi was. Immediately Bhima said: "Brother! You order me to bring Draupadi. I will bring her." Yudhistira gave permission. Bhima put his weapon on the earth and jumped up the sky and caught hold of the Gandharva's leg. The Gandharva realized that he could not escape Bhima. He thought that the lady who was not helpful to him was not useful to anybody. So, he threw Draupadi down. Observing this, Bhima asked Arjuna, the son (who was born as a boon given to a devotee) of God Indra, to catch hold of Draupadi. Arjuna promptly caught hold of Draupadi without any injury. This incident proves the willpower and strength of the Pandavas.

Arjuna was disguised as Bruhannala, while they were following their life incognito. In one incident Krishna asked Arjuna to act as a female. He gave him the name Bruhannala. While they were ready to follow their life incognito, Draupadi said that the wife and husband could call each other by pet names. She gave the name Gangnam to Yudhistira. She said, "I will give a name to Arjuna." Immediately Arjuna said, "Draupadi! You don't have to give me a name. Why, because Madhav alias Krishna already gave a name. That name is Bruhannala." (Vijay Channel on TV, *The Mahabharatam*, a daily serial)

But there is another version. Once, Indra invited Arjuna, his son to heaven. So Arjuna went to heaven. There Urvashi met Arjuna and asked him to have intimate relations with her. But Arjuna told her she was like his grandmother, and he could not be intimate with her. Urvashi got angry and cursed him to become an animal. Arjuna complained about this incident to his father, and he tried to convince Urvashi to take the curse off. But Urvashi said that the curse could not be reversed. Arjuna could utilize this curse for one year when he needed. In that way, he utilized this curse when the Pandavas were incognito.

At the time of Monarchy, if a king did Rajasuya Yagna he could declare himself an independent king. The Pandavas who were under the control of Drudarastra, wanted to become independent kings. So after Bhima succeeded Jarachand, Krishna wanted to do the Rajasuya Yaga. Yudhistira performed that. He invited all the kings. He also invited Duryodhana. The Indraprastha kingdom was built with the help of Maya. So it had many wonders like the palace that was built inside water. One flower girl welcomed the guests. While walking in the palace, in one place Duryodhana thought there was water. He walked carefully as if he was walking in the water. In another place, where water really was there, he walked in a carefree manner. So he fell down. Draupadi who was observing this laughed loudly. Duryodhana felt ashamed and also angry. At that moment he wanted to take revenge on Draupadi. But this was different from the scene which was broadcast on Vijay T.V.

Mathias's sons are Nakul and Sahadev. Sahadev is well versed in astrology. According to his dharma of occupation, even if his enemy asked about his future and there was something inauspicious supposed to happen, he had to forecast it without hiding the fact. Before starting the Bharata War some ceremonial activities like giving human sacrifices, finding the auspicious time for starting the war and so on, had to take place. Duryodhana first approached Sahadev and asked him to find the auspicious time to start the war. Sahadev told him if you start the war at full moon day, after giving a faultless human as a sacrifice, you will certainly win in the great Bharata war. Then he left. Immediately Krishna who was present there asked Sahadev whether he had paved the way for their defeat. And Arjuna's son Nallaravan is ready to become the sacrifice. Krishna asked them what they were thinking. He said that he was always looking out for them, for their victory. Immediately Sahadev told Krishna that he knew who he was; he knew Krishna was trying to destroy all the people in the world including them. So he told him not to talk as if he was working for them. Then Krishna asked Sahadev if he could stop the Bharata War. Sahadev said that the Bharata War could be stopped if they did certain things. Krishna asked what they were. Sahadev said that if they could turn Yudhistira into a sanyasi, send Bhima and Arjuna to the underground jail, cut Draupadi's hair and keep her in his heart, these would stop the Bharata War. Krishna laughed and said that as far as his people were concerned, they could do what they wanted, but he wondered how he could keep him in his heart. Then both of them went into one room. As soon as they entered the room, Krishna split into many figures and filled the whole room. Sahadev sat in the middle of the room and meditated saying, Krishna!!! Immediately all the split figures entered into Sahadev's mind. Sahadev controlled his breath. Krishna was inside his heart, and Sahadev felt breathless. He asked Sahadev to relish the experience. But Sahadev told Krishna he knew who he was: "You will kill all the people in the war including us. So if you promise to save me, my four brothers, Draupadi and one of the successors, then I will release you." Then Krishna promised him he would do that. Sahadev released him. Krishna asked Sahadev not to reveal this secret to anybody, and Sahadev agreed to do what he asked.

Pandavas ruled their kingdom happily. Once there was an invitation from Krishna saying he was not feeling well. Immediately Bhima and Arjuna said they should go and see Krishna. But Yudhistira not only refused to go to see Krishna, he also did not allow Bhima and Arjuna to go. However, Bhima and Arjuna persisted. Yudhistira then asked them not to touch Krishna if they wanted him to touch them. Then Bhima and Arjuna went to Dwarka. There they saw Krishna. As soon as he saw them, Krishna wanted to get up and sit. So he asked Bhima and Arjuna to help. But they refused to touch him remembering their brother's advice. Krishna asked them to give at least their Gada (a heavy decorated dome-like ball with a short handle) and bow. They did accordingly. Krishna took all their strength through their weapons. While coming to see him, both of them carried their weapons so easily. But after Krishna took their strength they could not carry their weapons. They placed them on their heads and reached their kingdom. Seeing this, Yudhistira asked them why they did not listen to his words. He felt their time was over. They should crown his son Parikshitu and leave the kingdom. They did that and then travelled to heaven. That is a different story.

In the Bharata War, Pandavas won the war. Yudhistira was crowned king and ruled. One day two farmers came with a treasure pot. Of the two farmers, one farmer had bought land from the other farmer. The farmer who bought the land found treasure in that land. That farmer went to the other farmer who sold the land and told him that he got treasure from the land he had sold him; so he said that the treasure was his. Immediately, the farmer who had sold the land said that he had sold the land to him, so the treasure was his. Both of them kept arguing. Then the case came to Yudhistira. He heard the case; he had to give the judgment for that case. So he asked them to come the day after. But the next day the Kalyug started. The king of Bharatavarsha now was Parikshitu. When the two farmers came, Parikshitu listened to the case. Then he asked farmer number one whether he had a son. He said he did. Then he asked the other farmer if he had a daughter. He answered in the affirmative. Parikshitu wisely advised them to get the daughter of the one married to the son of the other and give the treasure as a wedding gift to them. Both farmers felt very happy and praised the king. They left the king's court completely satisfied.

In the above examples of the stories that are still in the oral tradition, we can see some good stories that are a part of the culture and community of a country. Hope one day these stories would get written down and would be available to a larger audience. There are many such stories narrated in many communities in India, in many languages and dialects. It will be interesting to collect these and interpret them to find out how we all understand and interpret epics at the spoken level.

Bibliography

Datta, Amaresh (1 January 2006). *The Encyclopaedia of Indian Literature* (Volume Two) (Devraj to Jyoti).

Random House Webster's Unabridged Dictionary,

Oxford Dictionaries Online.

Murthy, S.S.N. (November 2003). "A Note on the *Ramayana*," *Electronic Journal of Vedic Studies*, 10 (6): 1-18.

Parimalagantham A., *Oral Stories Related to the Mahabharata*, www.languageinindia.com, Vol. 14.

Sundararajan, K.R. (1989). "The Ideal of Perfect Life: The *Ramayana*," Krishna Sivaraman; Bithika Mukerji, *Hindu Spirituality: Vedas through Vedanta*. The Crossroad Publishing, pp. 106-26.

CREATIVE WRITING

When the Mind Plays Tricks

ROSWITHA JOSHI
New Delhi

Middle-aged and on the fatter side, Mona lay in bed and tossed around, desperately trying to catch a few winks in the lap of the thick mattress a luxury hotel in Bordeaux offered. She wanted to be fresh for the long journey back to India, which would start at 4 o'clock in the morning, an ungodly hour anywhere, but more so in a country whose language she had failed to master. After decades of living in India she had retained no more than five words of French. Bonjour, oui, non, merci and merde; that was her spoken vocabulary. Her reading one was a bit better. At least it was enough to understand newspaper articles provided they were accompanied by tell-tale pictures.

Before she had left New Delhi for the South of France she had tried to brush up her French, but failed again. The melody of the language was just not in tune with her understanding of how a language should sound. Word separated from word, clearly distinguishable from each other like a row of individuals marching in line, not this singsong medley, or whatever one might choose to call it. She never managed to speak a sentence without giggling in between, at times for fun, at others to cover up her embarrassment.

Now the time to giggle was over and the time to worry on. She scratched her head till she felt blood on her finger tips. Her nose itched, so did her ears. She did not know where to scratch first. Her hands turned shaky, her palms hot and wet. What whirled like a dervish in her head was the question if and how she would manage to board the right bus from Bordeaux to the city of Toulouse, from where she was to catch her return flight.

What also whirled, though the room was her night dress. She had thrown it off, as the flimsy stuff was soaked in sweat. In a beam of moonlight that had pierced the curtain panels, she saw it dangling from the top of the TV screen. While squinting at it through tired eyes, it struck her that it looked like the remnant of a steamy tryst that had not taken place. A deep groan escaped her parched lips.

While she lay spread-eagled on her back to allow the draft of the air conditioner to cool the flesh of her overheated body, her feverish mind churned out image after image of Bordeaux's bus terminal, a place she had neither visited in person nor seen **in** pictures. Yet, whatever twisted and twirled before her mental eye was painted in strong colours with even stronger sounds infesting the air, a cacophony able to shatter even the best of ear drums. And hers did not even qualify as mediocre after a cracker had burst close to them at last year's Diwali celebration.

An urchin had aimed it right at her face, probably in retaliation for her expelling him from her garden paradise. A few months earlier she had plucked him from a lower branch of her mango tree by pulling his legs while the fellow stretched his arms to pick yet another fruit for his friends to catch. They stood at the other side of the compound wall eagerly awaiting the juicy missile. Face scratched, nose bleeding he fell into a bush, only to be pulled up and chased out by her. "I will get back at you," he had hissed while unceremoniously being flung onto the road.

From the mangoes in her garden Mona's mind jumped back to the bus terminal. Hustle-bustle movements started to flicker before her mental eye. They were as rowdy as the trailer of an Indian action movie. She saw lots of vehicles, some old and ramshackle, some new and brightly painted, standing in rows or, hooting and tooting, ambling in and out of passages in which people milled around, screaming, jostling, pushing to get in first, suitcases, bundles and all.

In the dim and hazy light of a very early morning or very late night – take your pick – she feared to be unable to read the signboards, shortsighted as she was, and ask for direction due to her limited French and unlimited nervousness. She imagined herself bubbling nonsense while rushing around, a weird apparition lost in a crowd where nobody bothered about her and men hung around with cigarettes dangling from cynical lips emitting columns of smoke that further fogged her vision.

What also agitated her was the memory of an incident that suddenly popped into her mind and refused to pop out. It lingered on like a stink that wrinkles the nose before it takes away the joy of breathing. It concerned Ina, a fellow German ex-pat and frequent travel companion, who was known for her curiosity and sense of adventure on one hand and her reliability on the other. Years ago, they had decided to discover India's south together and, living in different cities, join forces in Chennai to explore some temples and, once soaked in culture, digest their experiences lying on the white sands of a beach resort.

Mona had arrived well in time in the Chennai hotel of their choice and keenly awaited Ina's arrival. First she waited by impatiently walking up and down the garden path and then by looking out of the window of her room, a frown firmly fixed on her forehead, she waited for a long time. The minutes stretched into hours, the hours into darkness and then on and on. There was no sign of Ina and no message either.

For two days and the night in between she waited in vain, first wondering and then fearing what might have happened. The newspapers were full of stories of women being abducted, raped, robbed and murdered. Terrible possibilities raised their ugly heads; some of them were severed with a bloody trunk lying at their side. With the passage of time the images became so horrible that she could not sleep, eat or read.

The least troubling explanation was that Ina had fallen sick and not left Mumbai at all, or overslept and missed the flight to Bangalore where she was supposed to attend a wedding. Mona dialled her number, first calmly, then frenetically. Nobody picked up, and mobiles were not yet in circulation.

In desperation, she finally called a common friend who assured her that Ina was in good shape and had indeed flown to

Bangalore. He himself had dropped her to the airport. From Bangalore she would catch a bus to Chennai, because she loved to travel by road to watch the world pass by, the little things that added flavour to the travel menu in her words. He also gave Mona the name of the hotel she had booked in Bangalore. When Mona phoned, the receptionist told her that her friend had checked out in a hurry muttering that she had to rush to catch a bus to Chennai.

In the evening of the second day Ina finally arrived, her usually pale face blotched and flushed under a sweaty mess of dusty copper curls, her T-shirt and long pleated skirt creased and filthy. She did not smell of perfume either. Her lips trembled, her mouth opened and closed like that of a fish breathing its last after being hooked.

Shrunk into the softness of a couch in the hotel lobby, her red and watery eyes stared for a while at Mona, before she gained enough control over her mouth to whisper that she needed a drink, a strong whiskey to wet her dried up tongue. Shrugging her shoulders helplessly, she also managed a smile, half-apologetic, half covering up her desire to cry. She looked like she was on the verge of a nervous breakdown.

"What happened?" Mona asked, taking a sip of her large gin tonic. Sleeplessness and worry had taken their toll on her too.

"I caught the wrong bus and then got lost. I do not know where. Just imagine, I do not know where."

"What do you mean?"

"I jumped into a bus, which I thought was the one to Chennai, and fell asleep. I was so tired from all the partying. When a pothole shook me awake, I noticed that all the road signs were in local lingo, Kannada, Tamil, I do not know what. The scripts were different, full of circles and loops. None was in English. For a long time, I assumed - and then tried to convince myself - that I was on the right track. When, after hours, there was still no sign of a big town I got suspicious."

"What did you do then?"

"Well, I chewed on my suspicion. Only when it had already turned dark and the bus stopped at some place did I finally ask a guy who wore pants instead of a wrap-around whether we were heading for Chennai. In response he shook his head and rolled it from side to side, until it stopped rolling in the direction of another bus close by. I took it as sign that that this was the one I needed and quickly jumped boats. I jumped boats several times."

"Could you not ask somebody else?"

"I ask and ask only to get empty stares or helpless gestures. Nobody understood me. Ha! At every stop there were crowds, but nobody spoke English and I did know a bit of the local languages. I tell you, it was a nightmare. So many people milled around shouting at each other, but none to talk to, I mean in a meaningful way. It was just by fluke that I, finally, caught the right bus. Otherwise, I don't know what might have happened."

"You might still be erring around. Thank god you made it." Mona sighed before mumbling, "Well, waiting can also be killing." She gulped down the rest of her drink noticing that Ina's glass was already empty. Almost in unison, they asked for a refill. Both needed a couple of drinks to recover from their past nightmare and master the strength to create a better scenario for the future.

Years later, when Mona met Ina in Germany where she lived a retired life, her friend disclosed that she still had bad dreams about her meanderings in what she could only describe as 'somewhere' in Karnataka or Tamil Nadu. "That was the worst time of my life," she muttered shaking her by now graying curls as if she still had to get rid of some dust particles. Memories, just memories.

The future was about to start when after hours spent in a state of semi-wakefulness, Mona's alarm went off. She stumbled out of bed and peeped through the curtains. It was pitch-dark. There was no noise, no movement, even the moon was clouded. Well, she sighed, I chose this hotel for its quiet location. The hustle-bustle is soon enough to start. The thought of a bus terminal teeming with people, pushing, shouting, hurrying, hawking or just idly hanging around smoking, made her grin lopsidedly into the mirror. Her eyes betrayed her excitement. They gleamed almost feverishly.

She quickly dressed and pushed her vanity bag into the suitcase and then went down to the lobby, where the receptionist informed her that the taxi he had ordered the evening before was already waiting. "Fine," she muttered, paid her bill and rushed to the exit. An elderly driver heaved her suitcase in the boot and, panting slightly, opened the door for her. "Bus terminal," she said. "Oui," he listlessly replied, cigarette clenched between his teeth. And that was the end of their conversation, at least for the time being.

Face set as if carved in stone, he silently drove through streets that were bereft of life. There were no early morning joggers huffing and puffing at the roadside. There were no vehicles ferrying vegetables to the market, no pavement dwellers squatting wrapped in blankets or corpselike lying around, no overloaded trucks emitting stinking fumes. There was no noise, only darkness through which the road cut like a gleaming ribbon, and the humming of the engine.

The receptionist had told her that the drive would take about half an hour. As the minutes ticked away, she waited for the hustle-bustle she was used to in India, day in and day out, maybe reduced at certain hours, but definitely there. By now we should have reached, she mused, and anxiously peeped out of the window to see nothing but emptiness. Had the driver taken her for a ride? Abducted her?

Fear made her heart race. Unable to utter a word, she tapped him on the shoulder. He caught her frightened look in the mirror. "We almost there," he muttered while turning the car into a small lane, which ended at a red and white barrier. The little guardhouse at its side was empty. Behind it stretched a field, gray and uninviting. No soul was to be seen, only something bulky in the distance, which looked like the carcass of a huge animal. It reminded her of skeletons she had seen in the desert. Their meat had been devoured by vultures. The driver stopped the car.

"Why are you stopping here?" she asked.

"Bus terminal," he replied curtly, stepped out of the car and swung her suitcase from the boot onto the road. When she looked at him flabbergasted, he lifted it slightly and banged it on the ground again. "That's it," he nodded for emphasis.

"What are you doing? No, no. This cannot be true. This is no bus terminal. There is nobody." She looked around, panic written all over her face. A high wall threw a sinister shadow over one side of the field. She made out darkish patches on it. They seemed to move like shadows within shadows. "No, this cannot be true," she repeated shaking her head in disbelief.

"This is bus terminal," the driver now emphasized every word in a raspy staccato and, unmoved by her teary eyes, opened the back door and gestured her to get out. When she did not step forward but shrunk into the upholstery like a cornered animal, his face turned red with anger. "Get the hell out here! This bus terminal! I have other passenger." He tugged at her sleeve to show that he had no time for female wiles.

Her chest heavy with fear and fury, she gave up and, lugging her suitcase onto the pavement, stumbled onto the road, while he screech-turned the car and darted away. Now she was alone, alone as she had never felt before. The field looked as deserted as from the car window. There was no life. Not knowing what else to do, she moved ahead, feet leaden, head bent, shoulders slumped, dazed and lost in an inner world as bereft as the one outside.

Time ticked away. Were they minutes or mere seconds? When she finally raised her head, she saw a light in the distance. It came from an overfly bridge that was hazily illuminated and gleamed like a beacon through the mist of dawn. A motor bike swished by, then another. Should she try to get up there and hitchhike, she pondered and, nibbling at her lip, wiped the sweat off her forehead.

For a while she stood still to think how to get out of this god-forsaken place that jerk of a taxi driver had dropped her at like bird shit. The damn thing did not resemble a bus terminal at all. And then there was her flight to catch. Gosh, what a soup she was in!

Yet, just when she was about to give up hope to reach Toulouse in time or at all, she spotted headlights moving in her direction. They belonged to a car that stopped at the curb towards the end of the field. Two men got out. One of them parked a suitcase at his side, which she took as a promising sign. She took it as another promising sign that his burly figure resembled that of an old friend in India.

The men did not part ways immediately, but entered into a lively discussion, lightened by bouts of laughter. She watched them for a while and then quietly walked towards them.

"May I stand with you? I want to go to Toulouse," she shyly asked.

"Sure, the burly man," replied without so much as looking at her. "I will be going there too. The bus will reach in five minutes." She felt like she had hit the jackpot. The man was not only waiting for the same bus, but spoke English too!

"Thank you," she muttered and quietly waited for the five minutes to be over.

Exactly five minutes later, a bus emerged out of the haze and moved towards the wall. The moment it slowed down, the wall sprung alive. The sinister patches she had suspiciously ogled from afar turned out to be people who had either crouched against it or slept on the pavement below. They boarded as if in a daze. And she too clambered up the stairs to find the bus almost filled to capacity. She checked her ticket. Her seat number was 13. She had paid a little extra for it.

"Where is seat number 13," she asked pushing through the barely lit passage.

"Ha, ha, no seat numbers," a sleepy voice chuckled.

"But I paid for one," she mumbled.

"Then get off and take another bus."

"No! No! No!" She cried through a dense fog of memories and dropped down next to a girl, who was so fast asleep that she did not even notice that Mona had pushed herself into the slim space between her body and the window, finally a speck in a crowd, even if it was a small one.